TONI MORRISON

Anton Chekh...

T... ...y

Ivan **Turgenev**

Cervantes

sappho

ERASMUS

...oh

Fyodor Dostoevsky

Guy de Maupassant

...che

MY SOUL

HOPE ON A TIGHTROPE

Please visit:
Hay House USA: **www.hayhouse.com**®
Hay House Australia: **www.hayhouse.com.au**
Hay House UK: **www.hayhouse.co.uk**
Hay House South Africa: **www.hayhouse.co.za**
Hay House India: **www.hayhousecom.in**

HOPE ON A TIGHTROPE

WORDS & WISDOM
CORNEL WEST

SMILEYBOOKS

Distributed by Hay House, Inc.

Carlsbad, California • New York City
Sydney • London • Johannesburg
Vancouver • Hong Kong • New Delhi

Published in the United States by SmileyBooks

Distributed in the United States by: Hay House, Inc.: www.hayhouse.com • *Published and distributed in Australia by:* Hay House Australia Pty. Ltd.: www.hayhouse.com.au • *Published and distributed in the United Kingdom by:* Hay House UK, Ltd.: www.hayhouse. co.uk • *Published and distributed in the Republic of South Africa by:* Hay House SA (Pty), Ltd.: www.hayhouse.co.za • *Distributed in Canada by:* Raincoast: www.raincoast.com • *Published and Distributed in India by:* Hay House Publishers India: www.hayhouse.com

Design: Charles McStravick

Interior Photos: Grateful acknowledgment is made for the photographs from the following sources: Jefry Andres Wright, The Smiley Group, Fredrica S.Goodman, Kawai Matthews, Quillard Inc., and Cornel West.

Library of Congress Control Number: 2008930568

Hardcover: ISBN: 978-1-4019-2186-6

11 10 09 08   4 3 2 1

1st edition, November 2008

Printed in the United States of America

To my beloved children,

Clifton West and Zeytun West,

and my blessed grandson,

Kalen West,

in whom

I am well pleased.

CONTENTS

CHAPTER ONE

STATE OF EMERGENCY

We are now in one of the most truly prophetic moments in the history of America. The poor and very poor are sleeping with self-destruction. The working and middle classes are struggling against paralyzing pessimism and the privileged are swinging between cynicism and hedonism. Yes, these are the circumstances that people of conscience must operate under during this moment of national truth or consequences.

We have witnessed the breakdown of the social systems that nurture our children. Our rootless children—not just the one-out-of-three black, one-out-of-four-brown, and nearly one-out-of-three red children who live in poverty, but the one-out-of-five children in America who live in poverty. We are talking about the state of young souls: culturally naked, with no safe moorings, these children have no cultural armor to protect them while navigating the terrors and traumas of daily life. Young people need a community to sustain them, so that they can look death in the face and deal with disease, dread, and despair. These days, we are in deep trouble.

The audacity of hope won the 2008 Democratic primary, yet we are still living in the shadow of the vicious realignment of the American electorate, provoked by the media's negative appeals to race and gender and the right-wing propaganda that bashes vulnerable groups. The effects of the U.S.'s economic contraction that began in 1973 have only intensified in the new global economy. Even as deep-democratic struggles began in the mid-1990s in response to corporately controlled globalization, we faced an unprecedented redistribution of wealth from working people to the elite and the gutting of the nation into public squalor and private opulence.

Culture, in part, provides people with the tools and resources to steel themselves against adversity and convinces them not to kill themselves or others. This is the reason why I am preoccupied with a sense of the tragicomic. At the moment in which we must look defeat, disillusionment, and discouragement in the face and work through it—a sense of the tragicomic keeps alive some sense of possibility. Some sense of hope. Some sense of agency. Some sense of resistance. We have not been too successful in persuading people not to kill themselves or others: from the police homicide of Sean Bell in New York City to the torture and prisoner abuse at Abu Ghraib in Iraq, from street thugs to corporate thugs—people of color, women, youth, the working poor, gays, and lesbians are being targeted. I call it the gangsterization of America.

This is what happens in moments of cultural decay. This is what happens in moments of cultural breakdown. Moreover, to talk about cultural resistance at this time means to ask: How do we analyze this present moment and discern some sources of vision and hope? I look at culture from the vantage point of a black freedom fighter. We are not going to be here that long. Culture moves us—it helps create the structures of meaning, feeling, and purpose that keep the deep democratic tradition alive.

As bad as things are, we have faced worse conditions. We have always had courageous people willing to stand up and tell the truth, expose lies and bear witness to love and justice. We still have people who say they are willing to build on this tradition.

As our society faces deeper and deeper crisis, progressives are beginning to be heard again. People are looking to a variety of different voices and visions for leadership and direction, about how we can overcome these situations. For too long, Americans looked to the right. We have looked to neocons, Republicans, Reagan, Bush and Bush, Cheney and Rumsfeld. They have pulled us deeper into a dark, bottomless pit. Yet if people are interested in looking somewhere else, progressive possibilities are reemerging.

Such progressive formations have been the history of black folk. There was slavery. Then there was a Constitution that never used that word but counted black bodies as three-fifths of a man. While America was celebrating its liberty, 20 percent of the inhabitants of the 13 colonies were enslaved. In 1829 you had abolitionist David Walker saying that America will eventually have to deal with its white supremacist slavery. It will end up a house divided against itself, split down the middle with war and bloodshed. They said he was crazy. He was dead eleven months after he published the great *Walker's Appeal*. Thirty-some years later, his prophecy came to fruition. America had to come to terms with its white supremacy in the face of major catastrophes and war.

The Union won the war. White supremacy won the peace. After the Compromise of 1877, which ended Southern Reconstruction and began the era of Jim and Jane Crow, it was, "Here we go again!" From Frederick Douglass to Martin Luther King, Jr., sooner or later, just as you had to break the back of white supremacist slavery to save democracy, you will have to break the back of American apartheid or you will lose your democracy.

In the 60s, while black youths were being hosed down in the streets, black folk came to the rescue again. Dr. King and civil rights activists like Fannie Lou Hamer and Robert Parris Moses helped save democracy in America. There was the hypocrisy of America talking about freedom while oppressing black folk and noting that the Soviet Union had no freedom because it repressed and subjugated its citizens. Black folk came to the rescue.

What if they had killed Douglass in 1848? Or if Dr. King's house had been bombed a few minutes later in 1956? If Dr. King had returned early from that meeting with precious Coretta and the children, they would have all been killed. America would probably be much more authoritarian, if not crypto-fascist.

Now here we are in 2008. America finds itself looking to its blues people again to provide vision to a nation with the blues. That is a source of hope. Yet hope is no guarantee. Real hope is grounded in a particularly messy struggle and it can be betrayed by naïve projections of a better future that ignore the necessity of doing the real work. So what we are talking about is *hope on a tightrope.*

© The Smiley Group

CHAPTER TWO

COURAGE

It takes courage to interrogate yourself.

It takes courage to look in the mirror and see past your reflection to who you really are when you take off the mask, when you're not performing the same old routines and social roles. It takes courage to ask—how did I become so well-adjusted to injustice?

It takes courage to cut against the grain and become non-conformist. It takes courage to wake up and stay awake instead of engaging in complacent slumber. It takes courage to shatter conformity and cowardice.

◆

The courage to love truth is one of the preconditions to thinking critically.

◆

Thinking for oneself is based on a particular kind of courage in which you hold truth, wisdom, and honesty in high esteem.

The reason you want to think for yourself is because you understand that people often are not telling you the truth. When you place a high value on truth, you have to think for yourself.

◆

If you're unwilling to muster the courage to think critically, then someone will do the thinking for you, offering doublethink and doubletalk relief. People will apply a certain kind of pressure to push you into complacency and maybe even cowardice. It's not long before you rationalize, *This isn't really me. I don't* really *think this way . . . but let's go!*

◆

As crucial and precious as the intellect is, it can become a refuge that hides and conceals emotional underdevelopment, and diminishes your ability to think critically.

What we need at this particular moment is to bring together those who are willing to muster the courage to think critically, look at the basic assumptions of public discourse, and critique the way our history is told.

◆

When ordinary people wake up, elites begin to tremble in their boots. They can't get away with their abuse. They can't get away with subjugation. They can't get away with exploitation. They can't get away with domination. It takes courage for folk to stand up.

◆

American democracy is great precisely because you have had courageous, compassionate citizens who were willing to sacrifice, to think critically, and connect with others to ensure that the Bill of Rights has had substance, that working people have had dignity, and that people of color have a status that ought to be affirmed. Think of the courage that went into that!

◆

February is a serious month because we start talking about Sojourner Truth, Harriet Tubman, Frederick Douglass, and Martin Luther King, Jr.

And we can't talk about these freedom fighters without acknowledging white brothers like Elijah Parish Lovejoy, an 1834 graduate of the Princeton Theological Seminary. He was shot down like a dog by a pro-slavery mob because of his part in the abolitionist movement, fighting for a free press, and affirming the Bill of Rights.

Lydia Maria Child was a white sister who in 1883 wrote *An Appeal in Favor of that Class of Americans called Africans,* in the same spirit as David Walker's *Great Appeal.*

Asian sisters like Grace Lee Boggs. Jewish brothers like Harry Magdoff. Well-to-do white brothers like Paul Sweezy. Brown sisters like Dolores Huerta. Brown brothers like César Chávez. Red brothers like Russell Means. We can go on and on. This is what makes a democratic tradition strong.

The democratic tradition says what? "Whosoever will, let them come."

◆

It's critical to understand your history, and then be true to oneself in such a way that one's connection to the suffering of others is an integral part of understanding yourself. This is a deep problem these days. To be great in our times too often means to have great material prosperity and no moral magnanimity at all.

◆

If you don't muster the courage to think critically about your situation, you'll end up living a life of conformity and complacency. You'll lose a very rich tradition that has been bequeathed to you by your foremothers and forefathers.

◆

In America, when we talk about a catastrophe, we talk about indigenous people. We talk about slavery. We talk about women coping with patriarchy and domestic violence. We talk about gay brothers and lesbian sisters being taught to hate themselves. We talk about workers crushed by the capitalist elite. It is a view from the bottom up——through the lens of the cross.

That view is too often a minority view within the Christian community because it requires too much love, too much courage. Who wants to pay the ultimate cost like Brother Medgar Evers? People are too scared. I understand that. I still love them. I affirm Medgar's courage because he dared to look at the world through the lens of the cross and paid the ultimate price.

Malcolm did it in the Islamic tradition. Martin certainly did it in his tradition. He bore his cross from age 26 until he was assassinated at 39. The American Empire is just so cross-averse.

America denies its night side until it breaks right through. There's no direct reference to slavery in the original U.S. Constitution. That's not just a slight gesture. That's lying.

You can't get away with that. You end up fighting a civil war over an institution not invoked in the Constitution. That's a level of denial that's incredibly deep. You think you're innocent, yet you've created the catastrophe right in your midst. You try to sanitize and sterilize it so expertly that you think the funk is not going to hunt you down. But it never works.

◆

It is unclear whether we're going to make it. I'm not an optimist at all. Brother Barack Obama says he has the audacity to hope. I say, "Well, what price are you willing to pay?"

It's no longer enough to be willing to die. You have to be willing to live the truth. Somehow, you have to be able to walk that tightrope.

◆

We have too much cynicism around here. It's too easy. There's too much pessimism. Pessimism and optimism are the flip sides of the same coin. We should reject the whole coin.

When you're optimistic, you can stand apart to see how things are going. But when you're full of hope, you're in the midst of the muck. You're working it out with love power and a commitment to justice. Your unshakable connection to the story and tradition that shaped you is what sustains you.

We have to expose the social breakdown that produces the conflict that separates human beings from hope and courage and discipline and risk-taking.

◆

We need to be true to ourselves. I say that to Brother Barack Obama all the time. "This above all—to thine own self be true; And it must follow, as the night the day, Thou canst not then be false to any man."

To be true to yourself means finding yourself. This became something of a challenge for Sister Hillary Clinton. You need to have a self to be true to. You can find yourself, but what self is it? What's the substance of it? You can't discover it by simply checking the next poll.

And I'm not speaking just about Sister Hillary. This is what happens to most politicians. I pray to God that Obama is never reduced to that. American politics has a way of grinding the best out of a person. It squeezes their hope into cheap optimism. It reduces their prudent judgment into opportunistic behavior.

When Martin King was killed 40 years ago, something died inside all of us. If someone that morally sublime, yet human, could be murdered, that's not the stuff for sustaining people's sense of courage, struggle, and sacrifice. They begin to turn away and say, "My God, America doesn't have the capacity to treat the masses of black people decently or humanely."

Middle class Negroes may make the mainstream comfortable, but the mainstream isn't going to treat Tawanda and Tyree on the block the same way. That's who Martin stood for. He didn't stand just for middle class entrée into the upper echelons of society. He wasn't against it, but it was not what he stood for.

People say, "You know what, Brother West? I understand what you're saying. It's fascinating that you're still tied to the 60s, but I think I need to become more well-adjusted."

"Well-adjusted to injustice?"

"I wouldn't put it that way," they say "But you need to tone things down. You have too much rage and righteous indignation. I mean, you won't go Jeremiah Wright on me, will you? I need somebody to tone things down a bit for me to be able to go on about my business."

"Everybody has a different orientation," I reply. I don't believe everyone needs to have the same righteous indignation that I do. I'm a Christian, so I have Jesus in the temple. I have a martyr against the marketeers.

◆

9/11. Never in the history of the nation have U.S. citizens felt so unsafe, unprotected, subject to random violence, and hated for who they are. It was a new experience for many Americans.

I've had many white brothers and sisters come up to me. "You know, Brother West," they say, "I just can't get over this sense of being hated like this." I reply, "You don't say? Really?"

I say, "My dear brother, to be a nigger in America for 400 years is to be unsafe, unprotected, subject to random violence, and hated for who you are . . . we've got some experience that might be useful. We have some perspectives that might provide some insight."

Now that America, in this particular sense, has become *niggerized*, what kinds of resources are available? Will Americans become courageously Socratic and self-critical? Or will they become self-righteous? Will they become prophetic or vengeful? Let's look at certain moments in history when black folk had to respond with astonishing courage to the vicious form of niggerization called terrorism.

One of the most courageous moments in American history took place in 1955. Very few people want to talk about it. In August 1955, Emmett Till was murdered by his fellow citizens, a victim of American terrorism, his body thrown into Mississippi's Tallahatchie River.

Emmett Till's body was brought back to Chicago. The funeral resulted in the first major civil rights demonstration in the 1950s. It was three months before Rosa Parks sat down in order to stand up for justice in December 1955. Fifty thousand fellow citizens of all colors walked by to take a look at Emmett Till. His mother left the coffin open so that everyone could see.

It was Roberts Temple Church of God in Christ, where Mamie Till walked to the lectern. She looked over at her baby, whose head was five times the normal size, and she looked into the eyes of the black folk of South Side Chicago, and into the eyes of America.

Tears flowing, Socratic juices at work, she said what? *I don't have a minute to hate. I'm going to pursue justice for the rest of my life.*

What spiritual maturity, moral wisdom, care, and love went into that statement. It was rooted in something very deep. It was rooted in a decision to keep track of the humanity of the very people who had dehumanized her son. This was not some isolated occurrence. There was a tradition that produced Mamie Till. It took the questioning of dogma like white supremacy very seriously.

My God. How profoundly courageous! Here's a grieving mother speaking on her son's behalf and speaking for the best of her tradition. Martin King's in the background. Fannie Lou Hamer's voice is there. A. Philip Randolph's voice is there—and many nameless and anonymous black leaders who knew they would have to deal with situations in which they were unsafe, unprotected, subject to random violence, and hated for who they were.

◆

Think of the courage of Dr. Martin Luther King, Jr., when four young black girls in Birmingham became victims of American terrorism. It was the Sixteenth Street Baptist Church on September 15, 1963.

Brother Martin cried in public. He did not know what to say. He wondered if nonviolence was a hoax when people killed babies in Sunday school. He looked at the parents. Tears flowed again. What did he say? "Somehow we need to muster the armors of love and justice." Now that's a courageous people at their best.

◆

When we try to specify the various forms and varieties of the courage to love, we really have to ask, "Love for what?"

When we talk about the courage to love, to think for oneself, it rests on the courage to love truth. The love of truth, wisdom, and justice is not the same as loving individual people.

When you talk about the courage to love real people, there is certainly a truth in pain, sorrow, and grief. That truth is very different from the truth found in abstract theory.

◆

Now is the time for courage to love in a way that's not sentimental. It's a dangerous force that put Jesus on the cross. That's the kind of love I'm talking about. You can touch it. You can feel it. You know that you're empowered when you're connected with that kind of love. Grandma displayed exceptional dignity and grace to cope politically, spiritually, and lyrically while keeping a smile on her face. She worked at Miz Ann's house for over 42 years with no pension. But she was a queen on Sunday! That takes courage.

Where does that wellspring come from? It doesn't fall out of the sky. It comes out of a history of struggle. It comes from song, word, gesture, deed, family, institution, athletic networks, and musical apprenticeship. That's what has sustained us.

◆

Young people watch TV, hear from their friends, listen to the radio, and watch videos. Is that the truth? If you accept uncritically and blindly, then it's clear you don't really have a love for the truth. You have a love for what people tell you. Or it can be love for prevailing opinion. Sometimes we just fall in love with lies.

◆

Lies can generate some deep love. You can be addicted to lies and falsity as a way of dealing with life. You can fall for illusion, delusion, deception, and deceit.

◆

I'm concerned about the younger generation. Traditions are not something you simply inherit——you have to fight for them. You want to keep them vital, vibrant, and strong. You have to learn how to be their stewards. You have to be willing to sacrifice for them. You don't gain access to traditions by osmosis.

◆

Black people have never had the luxury to believe in the innocence of America. Although we've experienced the worst of America, we still believe that the best of America can emerge.

◆

The best that the prophetic tradition has been able to do on American soil is to produce a social movement. Yet every social movement was either crushed or absorbed. This is why it takes a tremendous act of faith and a tremendous act of courage to cut against the American grain—because the powers that be are very serious.

CHAPTER THREE

PHILOSOPHY

The word *philosophy* really means "philosophia," love of wisdom.

Anybody who has the audacity to embark on a quest for wisdom is really on quite an adventure because it requires a lot of courage, determination, discipline, and most importantly, humility. You have to be open to the voice, viewpoint, and vision of others.

◆

Any time you talk about wrestling with the terrifying question of what it means to be human, you must begin with the Latin *humando*, which means "burying." To be human is to bury your dead, to put those beloved corpses in the grave, and somehow connect yourself to them. To never forget.

◆

Wrestling with death, not simply as some event that's going to happen to you at the end of your life, but calling into question certain assumptions and presuppositions that you had before you arrived—that's learning how to die. That's what Plato himself said.

◆

Any time you surrender a prejudice or give up a presupposition, that's a certain death. To learn how to die in this way is to learn how to live.

◆

Paideia means "deep education"—learning how to die to live more intensely, critically, and abundantly. Because when you die, you give up certain assumptions and presuppositions to be reborn into a higher level of maturity.

Like falling in love—the old self dies, the new self emerges and merges into another self, grounded by the gift of grace. Paideia is the death that signifies rebirth. When I went to Harvard I had to be willing to die in order to emerge stronger—more courageous, perhaps more decent. Because in the end, love is the force that transcends death. All the rest is sounding brass and tinkling cymbals.

◆

Love of wisdom is a meditation on and preparation for death because it's in that death that you are able to go through a transformation where your education in the deepest sense— or what the Greeks called *paideia*—can occur. This cultivation of yourself and the maturation of your soul teaches you the difference between the frivolous and the serious, between the superficial and the substantial.

◆

What kind of human being do you want to be? What kind of legacy do you want to leave behind? What kind of witness do you want to bear? The prophetic question remains: Are you willing to be in solidarity with those whose tears are flowing? These are profoundly human questions.

◆

You're made in the image of God. You're a featherless, two-legged, linguistically conscious creature born between urine and feces. That's us. One day your body will be the culinary delight of terrestrial worms. You know that. Be honest. Put on your three-piece suit if you want to, but that's not armor against death.

The question is: Who are you going to be in the meantime, in this time and space? You don't get out of time and space alive.

◆

Martin Luther King, Jr. was one wave in an ocean that says, *I am willing not simply to live and die for an ideal. I'm willing to learn how to die while I'm alive, so I can live life more intensely and abundantly.*

◆

The life of the mind is about a sense of awe, wonder, openness, exploration. It's an adventure in exploring different views and viewpoints, different arguments and perspectives. There's a certain spaciousness that goes with it, an expansiveness of heart, mind, and soul that has its own exhilarating joy.

◆

There's something about American folk. They're so obsessed with comfort, convenience, and contentment. It's just like living in a hotel where the lights are always on. That's why the great novelist Henry James called America a "hotel-civilization."

There's no darkness, no despair, no dread, no suffering, no grief. It's just Disneyland. It's just having fun, smiling all the time, living in nice, manicured, deodorized, vanilla suburbs, as if there are no dark forces that are penetrating and saturating life wherever human beings go.

America is a death-dodging, death-ducking, death-denying civilization. This is what you would expect from a hotel civilization. Disneyland and Disneyworld have bragged that no one's ever died on their premises. Oh, so American!

◆

Where there is no death, there is no life. There's escape from life. It's fantasy. It's holding at arm's length all of those inescapable realities, like death, dread, disappointment, discouragement, and disenchantment.

◆

Black folk had to deal with social death for 244 years. When they sang, "Nobody knows the trouble I've seen. Nobody knows but Jesus," they are not talking about Disneyland or Peter Pan-like realities of innocence and purity. They're talking about human wounds, scars, and bruises, and still somehow being able to transmit and bequeath certain senses of grace and love to their precious children, even if they couldn't keep track of them as they were sold from one part of the country to the other.

◆

The culture of advanced capitalist American society, the culture of consumption, revolves around the market—around buying and selling. This process turns everything into a commodity and undermines value and meaning in the name of ever-increasing profit.

This is dangerous because in a marketplace culture, commodification—the ability to put a price tag on everything—dominates more and more spheres of human life. This creates an addiction to stimulation, which is necessary to keep the consumer-culture economy going. ("Terrorist attack? We'll show 'em. We'll protect the American way of life. We'll go shopping!")

The marketplace culture of consumption undermines community, undermines links to history and tradition, and undermines relationships. The very notion of commitment becomes more and more contested. Addictive bodily stimulation becomes the model for human relationships. We see it in the dehumanizing exploitation of women's bodies in the advertising industry. We see it in TV sitcoms and reality TV shows that are fueled by orgiastic intensity.

Crack is a perfect example. Crack is indeed the postmodern drug because it releases the highest level of stimulation known to the human brain. It can create sensations many times more intense than an orgasm. Crack, and its less demonized but equally destructive pharmaceutical relations, supports a culture that is addicted to overstimulation.

◆

The marketplace culture seems inescapable, unavoidable. The problem of the marketplace culture, like any other human creation or legal construct, is that it can be used for ill if there's no means by which individuals are rendered responsible or answerable. That's what democracy is all about: How do we hold each other accountable?

◆

If you're not spiritually, politically, morally prepared to deal with success, then a catastrophe can follow thereafter. In fact, it can blind you in your own quest for greatness. Because all you actually think life is about are these fleeting pleasures and these commodities. If you think you can possess your soul by means of possessing *things*, you've got moral constipation stalking you!

◆

The quest for wisdom for a black people who have been dehumanized, degraded, demeaned, spit on, rebuked, and scorned, and at the same time have come up with very creative responses and very strong forms of resistance to that dehumanization, has been a tumultuous journey.

To be a black philosopher means that your quest for wisdom is going to begin from the underside of modernity and the night side of American democracy. You want, on the one hand, to be true to the best of your roots, but you also want to be open to a number of different adventurous routes.

You're European, African, and American. You're partly premodern because you're tied to premodern texts like Hebrew scripture, the New Testament, or even African stories, but you're also very modern at the same time.

You're not just dealing with science and technology—you're dealing with claims about rights, liberty, freedom, and equality, ideals that we associate with the modern world.

In some ways, you find yourself in the modern world, but not of it because you've been excluded for so long. You find yourself in America, but not of it because you've been marginalized for so long. To survive, you must bounce back and forth. You become very fluid and flexible.

In some ways, you have an advantage because your world is so large and full of different dimensions that other philosophers may not have access to.

◆

There is a crisis of purpose among black intellectuals in general and black philosophers in particular. There has been a decline in the quality of public intellectuals and independent academics who can catalyze the larger conversation about the destiny of vulnerable individuals, such as the black underclass.

Reading Plato and Malcolm X becomes seemingly ornamental and decorative rather than substantive and engaging. It's nice to know a little Plato that you can invoke at a cocktail party when you're off relaxing and not making money. But there's no sense that what's at stake might be your very life, as Socrates and many others believed.

◆

The democratic tradition accents decency and dignity, freedom and equality, excellence and even elegance in certain instances. It can be—and should be—about the choices that human beings make and how those choices are connected to shattering narrow forms of provincialism or fundamentalism, whatever that fundamentalism is.

Democracy is all about dialogue, discussion, and critical exchange, bold speech, frank speech, but rooted in that burying—that dying to live more fully. Democracy contests fundamentalism—religious fundamentalism, free-market fundamentalism, secular fundamentalism. These are made accountable through democracy. It faces down narrow, exclusive perspectives that make it difficult to open our minds to alternatives.

◆

Democracies are predicated not simply on Socratic energy, the critical engagement, and examination of dogmas, but also on trying to shape a person's character in such a way that whether one is Christian, Jewish, Buddhist, secular, agnostic, or atheistic, you must have compassion for something bigger than your own egocentric predicament. You must be able to make connections across difficult boundaries. In a real democracy, it's hard to remain tribalistic or regionalistic in any narrow way.

◆

HOPE ON A TIGHTROPE

The road of inquiry is open to all travelers to the degree to which they are willing to allow their relative ignorance or naked power to be put in the spotlight.

> American history has always been
> an interplay between tragic thought and romantic impulse,
> inescapable evils
> and transformable evils.

To be a critic is to muster available resources to respond to the crisis of one's own time in light of one's view of the past.

◆

Every social issue has an ethical dimension. There is some value judgment built into every issue, some moral vantage point from which the world is viewed.

◆

The vocation of the intellectual is to turn easy answers into critical questions and to put those critical questions to people with power.

The quest for truth, the quest for the good, the quest for the beautiful, all require us to let suffering speak, let victims be visible, and demand that social misery be put on the agenda of those with power. So to me, pursuing the life of the mind is inextricably linked with the struggle of those on the margins of society who have been dehumanized.

◆

Many students remember that wonderful moment when you leave your classroom and realize that your world view rests on pudding. You've completely lost your footing across the board. All of the assumptions and presuppositions you learned from your family, neighborhood, partners, mosque, synagogue, or church can't sustain you any longer.

Darwin hurts. Toni Morrison shook me up. That's called education. You don't have to agree with Morrison or Darwin but you've got to engage them. You don't have to agree with Kafka. But if you can make it through *The Metamorphosis* and then just go off and have a taco at Taco Bell, something is wrong.

◆

You can't talk about trying to overcome something unless you get the lies out of the way. Truth is all about allowing suffering to speak. Suffering can't speak if the lies are suffocating that voice.

◆

Here's the bottom line: to be inspired by ordinary human beings made by God who undergo suffering but who have the courage to imagine a different future and are willing to fight for it, and to decide to fight along with them. That is prophetic thought and prophetic action as I understand it.

◆

If success is just an end and not a means to something else, then spiritual malnutrition and existential emptiness await you. Do you think that somehow you can stuff your humanity into your profession and your social function? Try it and see. No way!

◆

Humanistic intellectuals are being marginalized in our society by the technical intellectuals, such as physicists, computer scientists, and so on, because they receive funding from huge private enterprises, from the state, and from the military-industrial complex. Why? Because the products they provide are quite useful for a market-driven society.

◆

The debate about what constitutes postmodern culture is not a mere disagreement about the use or misuse of a phrase but rather a raging battle over how we define and conceive the role of culture in American society.

◆

Postmodern culture looks more and more like a rehash of old-style American pluralism with fancy French theories that legitimize race, gender, and sexual orientation's entrance into the new marketplace of power, privilege, and pleasure. This entrée is not simply desirable, it is imperative. The past exclusion of nonwhite and nonmale intellectual and artistic talent from validation and recognition is morally loathsome.

Yet it is easy to fall prey to two illusions: first, the notion that inclusion guarantees higher quality. Second, the idea that entrance, or opening the gates, results in a significant redistribution of cultural benefits. Inclusion makes possible new dialogues, new perspectives, and critical orientations and questions. Yet only discipline, energy, and talent can produce quality.

◆

Darwin's Theory of Evolution describes organisms interacting with their environment as a whole. Consciousness is just one brief moment within a larger organism. It is mind, body, and soul all tied together. Darwin is inescapable—even for Christians!

◆

Nietzsche says that the highest construct in his philosophic imagination is what he calls a "gay Socrates" or a philosopher who dances. Basically, it's a philosopher with a groove.

◆

Black folk make our entrée into the Western philosophical tradition with our voices. A philosopher who dances is not just acceptable and understandable, but is indispensible. Black folk come out of a history of a people who only had their bodies and voices. You can't separate our voices from our bodies.

◆

I'm never optimistic. From that angle, the evidence always looks undetermined. But I am full of hope. I never give up on any human being no matter what color, because I believe they all have potential. In that sense, it's a kind of blues-inflicted hope rather than a cheap American optimism that motivates me.

I am in no way
optimistic,
but I remain a prisoner
of hope.

CHAPTER FOUR

INDENTITY AND RACE

We have to get our stories right from the very beginning. Part of any discussion of race has to do with how we tell the story.

◆

The very discovery that black people are human beings is a new one. This question of what it means to be human affects each and every one of us. That's why all of us have so much at stake in black history.

◆

You certainly can't talk about what it means to be human in an African body without wrestling with slavery as a form of social death. For 244 years black folk had no legal status, no social standing, no public worth whatsoever—you were just a commodity to be bought and sold like a piece of property or cattle. How are you going to navigate yourself through this experience of social death?

◆

Morally, all racisms are the same. Historically and psychically, racism against people of African descent has been a targeted assault on black intelligence and black beauty, black capacity and black potentiality. When one thinks of anti-Jewish racism, which has inspired vicious pogroms and an indescribable Holocaust, one sees that the attack on Jewish intelligence is very different from the attack on African intelligence.

African Americans were three-fifths human—we were monkeys or rapists. Now we are projected as crack addicts or criminals. We have always been put in a position of having to defend our humanity, a circumstance that often prohibits an honest exploration of just who we actually are.

◆

White brothers and sisters have been shaped by 244 years of white supremacist slavery, 87 years of white supremacist Jim and Jane Crow, and then another 40 years in which significant progress has been made. The stereotypes still cut deep. Any white brother or sister who deeply revels in the humanity of black, brown, yellow, and red brothers and sisters must undergo a kind of conversion, metamorphosis, and transformation.

◆

We have to recognize that there is a radical continuity between the killing fields of the plantations, the bodies hanging from the trees, police brutality, the prison-industrial complex, and the Superdome in New Orleans after Hurricane Katrina.

◆

If you view America from the Jamestown Colony, America is a corporation before it's a country. If it's a corporation before it is a country, then white supremacy is married to capitalism. Therefore, white supremacy is something that is so deeply grounded in white greed, hatred, and fear that it constitutes the very foundation for what became a precious experiment in democracy called the U.S.A.

◆

Sister Condoleezza Rice said that "the United States has a birth defect." But black folk caught hell for a long time before the birth of the United States. A birth defect is not the same thing as a denial.

◆

Brother Barack Obama refers to ". . . this nation's original sin of slavery." No, the original sin was the dispossession, subjugation, and near extermination of the indigenous people prior to the founding of the United States. We must never allow black suffering to blind us to other people's suffering—in this case, our American Indian brothers and sisters, and especially their precious babies.

White supremacy—now that's the real original sin that grounds American Indian and African oppression. That's the precondition for a nation that could then be founded on the exploitation, subjugation, and hatred of African people.

◆

Black America has served as a kind of moral mirror for America.
Not because black people have a monopoly on virtue or are
always on the side of justice. Black folk are just as human as
anybody else—with ups and downs, strengths and weaknesses,
ignorance and wisdom.

It's the very notion that black people are human beings
that cuts against the grain. It's a revolutionary concept for
the West.

◆

In 1776, 20 percent of the U.S. population was enslaved. It's
crucial to see America not as the great city on a hill, or "the
last hope of earth," as Lincoln said. America must also be
seen as an Egypt. In the early 20th century immigrants from
around the globe looked to America for opportunity, while
Marcus Garvey was trying to lead black people out of America
and back to Africa. The image of black people wandering in
America's Egypt—that cuts against the grain.

◆

I was 11 years old and had never learned how to swim. So my dear track coach asked me to get into a swimming pool one day. I jumped in and all these white folk just started running away as if something bad had happened. I didn't know what was going on. I had impurified the pool, you see.

The question rose in me: Where does this notion of white purity come from?

◆

It was exciting and difficult for me to go to Harvard and Princeton. I became part of the first generation of young black people to attend Princeton's lily-white institution in significant numbers. Owing to my family, church, and the black social movement, I arrived at Harvard unashamed of my African-Christian-militant-decolonized outlook.

I acknowledged and accented the empowerment of my black style, mannerisms, and viewpoints, my Christian values, service, love, militant struggle, and my anti-colonial sense of self-determination around the world. I had a real sense that the world I came from had equal status with the highbrow academic humanist world that I had entered.

◆

To live for 244 years with no legal standing, no social status, no public worth, with only economic value means that the issue of self-identity alongside truth and justice remains central. That's why race still matters. Can America be truthful about itself and still pursue democracy?

◆

Race is the one issue that can bring down the curtain on American civilization. It has the power to generate levels of polarization that will make it difficult for us to communicate with one another honestly. It can generate levels of conflict that result in unprecedented chaos and disorder. It is our rawest nerve, most explosive issue, and most difficult dilemma.

◆

Immigrants who came to the United States didn't realize they were white until they got here. They had to be taught that they were white.

An Irish peasant, fleeing from British imperial abuse in Ireland during the potato famine in the 1840s, arrives in the States. You ask him or her what they are.

They say, "I am Irish." No, you're white.

"What do you mean I'm white?" Then they gesture toward a black man. "Oh, I see your point!"

This is a strange land.

◆

It's easy to think that somehow, because there's been relative progress for a significant number of black people, that there has been some kind of fundamental transformation. Therefore, we lose sight of the degree to which the history of New World Africans, in this hemisphere for 400 years, still affects us all.

◆

We want to speak to the realities of young brothers and sisters who are wrestling with self-hatred, self-doubt, self-violation, self-flagellation, and self-destruction.

You can see it in chocolate cities across the board. And the white supremacy inside of black people leads us to demean ourselves and devalue ourselves. We view ourselves as less beautiful, less intelligent, less moral. The niggerization of black people—the attempt to view ourselves as less than human and thereby require that we defer to white supremacist authority for 400 years.

Since the end of slavery
there has always been a black underclass.
What is significant now is the size of it,
the social gravity of it,
and the frightening and terrifying responses to it.

There has been a chilling realignment of the American voting public's attitude. Issues of race are now linked to public welfare so that when most government social programs are discussed by the media and politicians, they become unfairly associated with black folk and women.

◆

Class now plays a crucial role in terms of limiting life chances for black kids and black people. Gender is also a very important factor. Though the reality of racism and exclusion is undeniable, racism is not the sole problem. Usually, when Americans talk about race, they are not talking about race in any kind of serious, historical manner. Race is one very crucial and undeniable variable in American society but it is inseparable from economic class and gender.

◆

Interaction between the sexes in the black community is unintelligible without highlighting the racist and poverty-ridden circumstances under which so many blacks live. Machismo is itself a bid for power by relatively powerless and degraded black men. Remember, too, that the white perception here is principally informed by interracial relations between black men and white women, relations in which black machismo is particularly pronounced.

There is an expectation among large numbers of white folk that black men be macho, and black men then tend to fulfill that expectation. Those who do not are perceived as abnormal. A crucial part of this phenomenon is the question of sexual prowess: if you're not a "gashman," your whole identity as a black male becomes highly problematic.

◆

One of the most disturbing things about identity talk—especially in America, but it's true around the world—is that when people speak about identity, they always begin by talking about the victims.

Having a conference on race? Bring on the black folk. We don't want to invite some white racists so they can lay bare the internal dynamics of what it is to be a white racist. No. Having a conference on gender? Bring on women.

Whiteness is as fundamental to the discussion of race as blackness is. Maleness is as fundamental to the discussion of gender as femaleness is. We need to get a handle on how this whiteness, maleness, and straightness functions over time and space in relation to blackness or brownness or yellowness or womanness or gayness or lesbianness.

◆

In America, human beings primarily define themselves physically, socially, politically, and sexually in terms of whiteness and blackness, maleness and femaleness, heterosexuality and homosexuality, and American and un-American. This is how we perceive ourselves, and it reinforces constraints on the human capacities of those who are victimized by the racism, the sexism, the homophobia, and the chauvinism.

◆

We have got to come up with mature forms of black self-love, black self-respect in which whiteness is not a point of reference, either negative or positive.

◆

There have always been class divisions in black America, going back to the division between slaves on the plantation. There were house slaves versus field slaves.

The difference was that black people always had a strong sense of "we" consciousness. We were all grouped together by the white supremacist authority and power in place at the time.

Even during the time of Jim and Jane Crow, you had deep class divisions, just like you had huge divisions in terms of color—the light-skinned black folk were able to gain access to certain opportunities that the dark-skinned black folk could not.

◆

The black middle class in the United States has become drunk with the wine of the world—materialism, narcissism, and hedonism. And then we wonder why the younger generation does not have access to the traditions of the struggle. Preach to young folk to be successful rather than to be great and they will think it's all about success.

Do you really believe that Sojourner Truth, Harriet Tubman, Marcus Garvey, A. Philip Randolph, and Malcolm X died so that you can just be successful? Do you think they died so that you can just be peacocks, walking around saying, "Look at me, look at me, look at me!" Somebody needs to remind everyone that peacocks strut because they can't fly.

In America they shoot eagles and applaud peacocks, which is another way of saying that all that materialism—the clothes, the cars, the houses, the mansions, the status—is nothing but the paraphernalia of suffering, an attempt to distance yourself from the suffering because you have had so much of it.

◆

According to a 2007 Pew Research Center survey, 37 percent of black folk don't consider themselves as part of a single black race. The "we" consciousness of black people is waning in a significant way. If that's true, it means that it may become much more difficult for certain black middle class people to feel as if the black underclass warrants a focus and concentration.

Instead they can accept the more mainstream, assimilated perspective, which is that the black underclass is not a black underclass at all. It's just individuals who are lazy, undisciplined, and haven't done their work. They get what they deserve. That's a common American mainstream perspective of the poor as a whole.

Once we lose any sense of a black upper or black middle class or a black upper working-class connecting with the black underclass with a "we" consciousness or sense of community, it becomes much more difficult to focus on the plight of the black poor.

◆

One of the distinctive characteristics of black folk is that we've been willing to be on intimate terms with death without allowing death to have the last word. In the face of the social death of slavery, the civic death of Jim Crow, the psychic death of self-hatred, the spiritual death of self-destruction, we have survived with a smile on our face, love in our hearts, and hope in our soul.

◆

The black freedom struggle is the key that unlocks the door to America's democratic future. It is the litmus test of American justice. The future of America is black because the deep meaning of democracy is to be found in Martin Luther King, Jr., connected to Frederick Douglass, connected to the best of the Black Panther Party, and connected to Ella Baker. This heritage shows what the true meaning of democracy ought to be if America dares to shed its ambitions and actually allows democratic possibilities to be realized.

◆

From the very beginning Obama said his candidacy was a sign that America was coming to terms with the vicious legacy of white supremacy. He's right about that.

The very fact that a black man could not just galvanize but actually convince fellow white citizens to go in the booth and not just vote for him but come out with a smile—that is significant. We don't want to downplay that. If he were to in some way say, "I've got to hit this issue head on and be more explicit," would that undermine the earlier strategy that allowed for those white brothers and sisters in Iowa and New Hampshire to come out for him? It's a tough question.

◆

On the one hand, my dear Brother Barack in the White House would be the great example of the American Dream come true. On the other hand, it could be the grand exhaustion of the dream built on the success of any one individual. The juxtaposition of a brilliant black man in the White House and suffering poor people along with the downward mobility of the middle class reveals the bankruptcy of a narrow American Dream.

◆

We live in a country where our understanding of racism is so impoverished. We don't even have a language to get at what's going on. You have so many white brothers who say, "When I hear Mr. Obama, he doesn't make me feel white and I love that. He just makes me forget I'm white." They think that's a compliment. Can't we be pro-humanity and embrace our colors and cultures?

There is an element of truth in terms of being not so much post-race, but just being in a moment in which white fellow citizens are willing to look at qualifications and vision as opposed to pigmentation and color. That's a breakthrough. To be anti-racist is not to be colorblind but color-embracing— even lovestruck with each other!

◆

Barack Obama actually becomes a kind of lightning rod. The old civil rights leaders are very suspicious because he hasn't gone through the struggle and doesn't have the scars that we have. Thank God! That's why we went through it. I don't want my son and daughter to have the same scars and bruises.

When they come up with a different analysis than I do, what am I going to do? Trash them? No, I just tell them, "I think you're right here. I think you're wrong there." They come back, "No, you're old school. You're right here. You're wrong there."

This is how Socratic dialogue proceeds. That's how it ought to proceed within the black community, within the larger white community, brown, yellow, red, and so on.

◆

The debate about whether Obama is black enough is a sad thing, given the crucial role mass media played in driving the distortions. In the black press, it was never a question of phenotype at all. It had nothing to do with his loving white mother or his brilliant African father.

"Black enough" always means "bold enough." Clarence Thomas is phenotypically, beautifully black. He's not bold enough.

He's a right-wing conservative who sides with the strong against the weak. That's not popular in the black community.

It's a question of principle. Thurgood Marshall was a beautiful high-yellow black. He was black enough because he was bold enough. He didn't side with the strong, he sided with the weak. Black people appreciate that. Not because we have a monopoly on truth, but because we come out of a history in which we look for heroic people in high places who side with the weak against the strong, whatever color they are. It's a matter of principle.

You look in the white press and they're asking, "Should Obama deny his mother?" What are you talking about? Adam Clayton Powell looked like a Puerto Rican, throwing his hair around as straight as his hair was! Black people loved him. How come? He was bold enough, which made him black enough. It's a very different kind of discourse.

Dr. West,

"Pa Moja Tuta Shinda!"
"Together We Struggle!"

I greet you in the tongue of our ancestors. My name is Randolph Knox and for the past 13 years I've been incarcerated in the State of New York serving a sentence for what seems like forever and a day for manslaughter and deadly use of a firearm. I won't downplay my criminal lifestyle nor will I sugarcoat my résumé to receive any sympathy from you. That is not my objective with this missive. Before I entered the penitentiary I was a bad man who had done some good deeds in my life. It's as simple as that.

After several years of going through a whole bunch of bullshit in this nightmare, my comrade gave me your book *Race Matters* to read. From the moment I finished it you became a great black figure in my eyes, along with David Walker, Nat Turner, Denmark Vesey, Malcolm X, and a few others that I admire. I know that you're not as great as those men were, nonetheless you are a black man I look up to. I'm sure you're praised by a horde of people in a better social position than me, but you'd be hard pressed to find anyone in your circle of admirers with the courage of a lion and the heart of a warrior that's willing to sacrifice the approval of their white colleagues for our struggle.

Don't get me wrong—I'm not one of those new black revolutionaries running around chanting "Death to Whitey!" Although I know the evil of whitey, my beef is with black folk like Clarence Thomas, Condoleezza Rice, Oprah Winfrey, and Armstrong Williams. They know better but refuse to do better. I call them agents provocateurs.

In fact, being from the city I never experienced real racism until I entered prison and was shipped up north to the mountains, where I got a taste of some real live sadistic cracker correctional officers. That's when I realized that there were two kinds of white folk. If you're not smart enough to differentiate the two by the time you're released, you can really leave prison hating white people. Luckily, I haven't reached that level and hopefully I never will.

Anyway, enough about that. I'm writing you today to ask you one question, and although it's personal I'm hoping that you will answer it truthfully.

As you know already (and if you don't), the penitentiary is flooded with know-it-alls, assholes, and a few scholars sprinkled in. It's absolutely amazing the shit I go through in here every day. Anyway, one day I'm in Attica yard talking the usual Sunday prison topics, "Fuck Whitey!, Black Power!" blah, blah, blah. When I mentioned your name and the books you've written, one of your detractors immediately shot you down, discrediting your thoughts on black unity and the black struggle because he claims that you are married to a white woman. Blasphemy!

I quickly came to your defense with this scoundrel by telling him to prove it. Of course he could not so he proceeded to lie and although I've never seen your wife I called him a liar. I told this fella that, based on the contents of your books and your views on the black struggle in America, it is unlikely, but not impossible, that your wife is Caucasian.

One thing led to another and things became physical between us. I know, this is probably the dumbest shit that you've ever heard in all your life, but I assure you not only is it the truth, it is quite serious. I curse myself every day for indulging in this stupidity, but when you're in this environment you can't escape the nonsense all the time. 95 percent of all arguments in prison stem from something extremely trivial, but then it turns into violence because personal insults are spewed back and forth and then it becomes a matter of disrespect, and before you know it someone is in the infirmary and the one is in the box talking about "It was his mouth." HA! HA!

I want to apologize for bothering you with this pettiness, but I have to know. Are you married to a white woman? Being that I came close to death or a new charge behind you and wifey, it's only right that I should know.

Thank you for your time, patience, and anticipated cooperation on this matter. I await the truth!

Respectfully yours,
Randolph Knox

July 10, 2007

My Dear Brother Randolph Knox,

Thank you for your powerful and poignant letter. Your brilliant intelligence and deep commitment to our struggle are manifest in your lucid words. I also was moved by your spiritual maturity and courageous honesty.

As to our brother—my detractor—who claims I am married to a white sister, please let him know he is wrong. I have not been married for years. My deep allegiance to truth and justice means that my life is not my own—so most of it is spent speaking (over 120 speeches a year), writing (17 authored books and 13 edited books), rapping (3 albums), organizing (with different political and religious progressives) and supporting my family (especially my precious mother, sisters, son, and daughter).

I indeed have been married—three times!—to a strong black woman (mother of my proud son), a sweet Puerto Rican woman and a beautiful African woman from Ethiopia. All three sisters enriched my life. I also have a precious daughter from a brilliant Middle Eastern woman whom I never married. Tell our dear brother that as a free black man who is willing to live and die for truth and justice—especially for black freedom and black people—I ask no one for permission as to whom I love or even marry.

We know that Frederick Douglass was married to a white woman. So what? His contributions to our struggle are immeasurable. And many black agents provocateurs are married to black sisters. The keys in life are the depth of your love to everyday people—so you sacrifice much—and the quality of your service to ordinary folk—so you treat them with respect!

As a progressive Christian in the grand tradition of David Walker, Ida B. Wells-Barnett, Martin Luther King, Jr., and Fannie Lou Hamer, I choose the way of the cross that speaks the truth, exposes lies, and bears witness for justice. And as you know, Brother Randolph, you never let detractors get you off track in your calling to our higher cause.

You just keep loving folk, fighting injustice, and swinging like Muhammad Ali and Sarah Vaughan. Stay strong!

Love,
Cornel West

CHAPTER FIVE

FAITH

I stand fundamentally on the profoundly Christian notion that we are each made equal in the eyes of God. A single mom on welfare has the same status as a corporate CEO and they both have the same right to human flourishing regardless of race, regardless of religion, nation, or gender. It is a deep, spiritually based notion of equality.

◆

Behold, that first century Palestinian Jew was born in a funky manger. He had some funky working-class parents sometimes dealing with unemployment and underemployment. He walked on some funky and dusty roads, didn't he? He brought together 12 funky folk. He didn't go out 100 miles to the vanilla suburbs, did he? He picked them right from around where he came from. It's so easy to forget the funk in Jesus's life because our churches can become so easily deodorized.

The funky gospel of funky Jesus can become so Americanized that it is reduced to marketplace spirituality, prosperity gospel, and Chamber of Commerce religion. No! We want to keep focused on the funk of Jesus, especially that funky blood at that funky cross.

If you don't find joy in serving others, if you don't understand the joy in loving people, then come back to the cross. Get down in that funky blood and understand what it means to be at that funky tomb that was empty when that prostitute Mary Magdalene showed up and had a message for the world.

You can't be committed to that kind of funky gospel if you're not willing to pay a price. You need to be willing to bear a burden. You need to cut against the grain.

Every religious tradition has been tied into various forms of domination and subjugation. Every religious tradition has been manipulated and bastardized by elites to try to control believers. At the same time there are always prophetic elements, dimensions, and slices of religious tradition that stand in opposition to the powers that be.

Christianity itself comes out of prophetic Judaism. Persecuted early on, Jesus ended up on the cross. This unarmed truth and unconditional love in the face of catastrophic circumstances was seemingly crushed, but the love bounced back. That story is what has attracted black folk—and others.

When we feel like we are being crucified every day like that first century Palestinian Jew crucified at Calvary, we hold on to that unarmed truth and unconditional love. It looked as though Jesus couldn't bounce back. Black folk have been locked into that long Saturday after Good Friday. We ain't had Easter yet. All we have is each other, and the promise of Easter, the promise of freedom.

◆

Constantine was the Emperor of Rome during the early years of Christianity. He took the underground religion that was persecuted and made it a state religion. Then he persecuted all other religions, and thereby forced Christianity on the population to make religion a weapon of the Roman Empire.

In these days of modern Constantinian Christianity, the blood of the cross has been transformed into Kool-Aid, and many are dipping in for upward mobility. It is a very different way of talking about spirituality. That's the truth not just for Christianity, but for religions across the board.

◆

Black people were moved by the image of the God of history who sides with the oppressed and the exploited—a God who affirms one's own humanity in a society that attacks and assaults black intelligence, and black beauty, and black moral character through white supremacist ideology. This message spoke to black folk very deeply.

There was also a political reason that black folk held fast to Christianity. Through its message, black people could engage in a critique of slavery, of Jim Crowism, of second-class citizenship, while holding on to the humanity of those whom they opposed. This is the great lesson that Martin Luther King, Jr., who is a product of this tradition, taught us.

◆

At its best, religion can provide us with vision and values, but it doesn't provide the analytical tools. One doesn't look to the Bible to understand the complexity of modern society. It can give us certain insights into the human condition, certain visions of what we should hope for, but we also need social, political, and economic tools.

◆

The spirit of the Lord still empowers those who have been cast aside to struggle and to not lose hope. It is this spirit that supports those who care for the socially invisible and politically marginalized.

◆

The black church has always had a prophetic wing that was critical of the powers that be, and a priestly wing that had to negotiate with the powers that be. They had to be deferential to survive. This tension is part of any religious tradition, and it's true for the black Christian tradition as well.

◆

The priestly black church tended to be a highly niggerized black church where the black pastor, although often eloquent, was so scared and intimidated by the white supremacist power structure that he was subordinate to it. This is why when King started his movement he knew that he would only get roughly 10 or 12 churches out of 85, because the other 75 were just scared. They'd been niggerized to the core.

They said, *Look, you don't mess with the white power structure. These folks will crush you. We're not going to win. We can't work together.* They said all the different things that come out of the colonized, niggerized mentality. It's understandable, but it's not justifiable.

The prophetic tradition that Martin was trying to galvanize in Montgomery said, *No, we're going to fight this thing. We want to de-niggerize Negros. We're going to shake the nigger out of them. Quit being scared. Walk. Quit being intimidated. Stand up. Quit walking around laughing when it ain't funny and scratchin' when it don't itch. Be a human being.*

◆

Standing for love and justice means you must straighten your back up. Martin Luther King, Jr., said, ". . . Whenever men and women straighten their backs up, they are going somewhere, because a man can't ride your back unless it's bent." That's a hard message because people had to pay a price. What he didn't add was, when you start walking, you can get crushed, go to jail, or get killed.

That's what it means to pick up your cross. That's what it means to fight with dignity. We don't want to romanticize the black church here. We're talking about the prophetic, de-niggerized church.

◆

Freedom is always a process because no one of us is fully de-nigger-ized in America. For the last 40 years, we've been under right-wing rule in this country just as for 400 years we've been niggerized.

◆

The prophetic church still remains, but it has become much weaker. It just couldn't deliver. It could talk and tell the truth, but to deliver it had to have some relation to the powers that be, and those powers were deeply conservative and right wing.

◆

American Christianity, in many ways, is a market form of Christianity. It's all about identifying with a winner. That's why Easter Sunday the churches are full, but Good Friday they're empty. Constantinian Christians like to show up when the victory is won.

Don't tell them about the main protagonist—Jesus—being treated like a political prisoner by the Roman Empire. Don't tell them about a senseless death based on injustice with greed, hatred, and fear trying to crush truth and love!

◆

In the 60s, we saw Christians engaging in anti-racist struggle, as with Martin Luther King, Jr., and later the with various black liberation theologians, like the great James Cone. In each instance, Christians were called forth to plunge to the depth of their understanding of the Christian gospel, which affirmed the dignity and sanctity of each and every individual. But these kinds of Christians were always a minority.

◆

For Christians, the problem of evil means: How does one respond to, and resist all forms of evil, especially institutional evil?

Christians must seriously consider sin on both the personal and institutional levels. In fact, grappling seriously with institutional sin has allowed me to arrive at some very radical democratic values—such as the need for accountability for all of us.

Democracy goes hand in hand with Christian faith.
You have an ethical obligation as a Christian
to fight for equal rights for all.

Prophetic thought has to do with putting your life on the line, with the help of your faith. True faith means you are not looking for a quick fix or a victory overnight. You do the right thing regardless of the consequence—because you want to be a decent and compassionate person before you die!

◆

A Christian should be able to go to the White House, a crack house, their momma's house or any house and come out with their integrity, vision, compassion, and commitment to justice intact.

If the Kingdom of God is within you, then everywhere you go you should leave a little heaven behind. People will know you to be a heaven leaver. You can learn to love your crooked neighbor with your own crooked heart because you're connected to a power and grace greater than your ego.

◆

The very notion of humane treatment is inseparable from the historic struggle for love and justice. Humane treatment four hundred years ago was very different from what it is now. Thus, the Christian has a mandate to identify with the downtrodden, the dispossessed, the disinherited, the exploited, and the oppressed.

> To be a Christian
> is fundamentally to live a sacrificial life,
> a love-informed life, a life of caring,
> and a life of giving.

People tend to think that religious talk is different from political talk. You can talk about the kingdom and say it's just a metaphor. But actually, it's very real. You have to have deep, deep religious faith to stay in the struggle for a long time. Ask anybody who's been in the struggle for the long haul. You have to have deep faith. Faith is our primary source of empowerment. If you haven't dealt with the bondage of death and despair, then you're going to be disillusioned after the first laps. This is not a sprint. This is a marathon.

◆

Since America is well-adjusted to injustice, the flag is no longer subordinate to the cross, the cross has become subordinate to the flag. In the end, the blood at the cross that ought to serve as a critique and judgment for all human beings becomes Kool-Aid. It serves as a refreshment for those in search of the American dream, of living large in some vanilla suburb, and enjoying a certain kind of status and power.

Any time you make the cross subordinate to the flag, you have idolatry. Americanized Christianity is shot through with forms of idolatry, making it difficult for people to keep track of the blood at the cross, the need to love, sacrifice, and bear witness to something bigger than nation, race, or tribe.

◆

As the right-wing political Ice Age begins to melt, the prophetic possibility inside the black prophetic church may begin to erupt. Reverend Jeremiah Wright is one example. He terrifies the white mainstream. When he says, "Not God bless America, God damn America. That's in the Bible, for killing innocent people." The white mainstream only hears, "God damn America!"

They say, *He's so unpatriotic, he's so ungrateful . . . he's a hate-monger. Why does he hate America?*

Any God worthy of worship condemns injustice anywhere. To be anti-injustice in America is not anti-American! If to condemn injustice in America is to be anti-American, so be it. To be Christian requires being maladjusted to injustice, which is the bottom line.

◆

One reason why the Garden of Gethsemane is so very important is because, even though God comes into the world in human flesh to love, serve, and die, even God had to choose.

Jesus said, "Let this cup pass from me." He still had to choose to have his will conform to the will of God. The greatest living Christian preacher—Gardner C. Taylor—has a grand sermon called "Gethsemane: The Place of Victory." Once you get humanized, fleshified, and concretized in space and time, you are in a choice-centered reality. To be human means choosing to have the courage to think, love, hope, and fight for justice and freedom.

◆

Gratitude always pushes out ego. When all these other folk are coming at you tooth and nail, you can look them in the face and say, "You're not going to make me bitter. You're not going to make me bigoted. I have work to do in the little time I'm here. I have a smile on my face because I've been so blessed." Thankfulness and praise don't provide the self with a whole lot of space for the ego to operate.

◆

When I went on that operating table for cancer surgery, I was thinking of all the unbelievable blessings that I've received in my life. I didn't know whether this was going to be my death or not. I had to wait to see what was going to be. But I refused to let death come in like a thief in the night and steal the joy and love I had already given and received.

◆

A lot of people believe in God, but they don't have a gracious disposition and don't put a premium on gratitude. Maybe it's because in their lives they think they have very little to be thankful for. Belief in God is inseparable from gratitude and graciousness.

In the end, your life will be
measured not by what you have.
It will be measured by the fruit you bear and the life you live.
It will be measured
by what kind of love
you really have.

If the churches and religious institutions fail, then the spirit will go somewhere else because the rocks will cry out if they don't.

◆

I'm first and foremost a Christian. But I'm a Christian who works through Anton Chekhov, through John Coltrane, through Toni Morrison. These prophetic artists understand that the tragi-comic character of the world is such that suffering, pain, and grief sit at the center of our reality. Upon this terrain we struggle to preserve our compassion, no matter what.

◆

As an intellectual with this Christian baggage, I'm going to be free because the world is not going to determine who I am. I'm in the world but not of it. I'm free to do what? I'm free to love across the board.

As you speak a truth, you can do it with a generosity, but also with a bite. So you can speak the truth, expose the lies— but most importantly, you can bear witness.

◆

It's impossible to talk seriously about fundamentally transforming America without talking about forms of spirituality. Spirituality is all about how you deal with your constraints and limitations. When you run up against constraints and limitations, you're going to need something to fall back on. You need a community that's sustained by a level of spirituality that contests, shares, and supports people— so that you don't become a short-term freedom fighter.

◆

God, no matter how powerful, cannot do two things: commit suicide or make a good soul. God creates human souls and those souls have to choose to be good.

There's always that strong element of real choice, decision, and commitment in Christianity. We're not machines or automatons. We have to choose to be Christians, choose Jesus, choose the good, choose justice, and so forth.

◆

Prophetic churches, prophetic mosques, prophetic synagogues can all play a fundamental role in nurturing children by transmitting noncommercial values. I'm talking about love, care, service to others, sacrifice, risk, community, struggles for justice, and solidarity. All of these nonmarketplace values struggle against a market-driven culture.

◆

Under that American terrorism called slavery, we sang, "Wade in the water . . . God's gonna trouble the water . . ." You've got to be in trouble to be transformed. If you do not have the courage to be where the crisis is, where the catastrophe is, you will never be changed.

We live in the American Empire
where the market-driven way of life,
the obsession with things and commodities,
has produced
a Constantinian Christianity in America.
It is a very market-driven Christianity—
the prosperity gospel,
an obsession with blessings in the form of Lexuses.
You go to some churches and see two ATMs
before you see a cross.

We have to critique the marketplace influences in the church so that the content of the gospel doesn't get flattened out. So that the message of the cross doesn't become diluted. So that the preacher doesn't become just another businessman.

◆

There's nothing wrong with being successful. There is nothing wrong with money. There is nothing wrong with power. The question is—is it connected to something bigger than you? Is it connected to what God wants you to do?

Is it connected to the prayer, not the petition you ask God for? Not the "let's make a deal" prayer, but the prayer that is, "Let thy will be done." Don't remove the mountain, Jesus—give me the power to climb the mountain. I can make it because I know you are with me. You promised to be with me always, even until the end of the world.

That's the kind of faith we're talking about.

CHAPTER SIX

FAMILY

All of us are our momma's child and our daddy's kid, whether we like it or not.

Family is a major vehicle through which history and memory can be preserved in the face of a culture that defaces history and erases memory.

Real family signifies a high level of compassion and intimacy between people. A compassionate family affirms the best of who you are even in the worst of circumstances. Even when you go to jail, your mama, sister, brother, or loved one will still believe in you because they know you can be better than whatever crime you committed. They don't give up on you and keep giving you another chance.

Intimacy and compassion are important too because they allow people to open themselves, take risks in relationships, and thereby allow the worst and the best to be seen. It's knowing that when people see the worst, they'll still be accepting. When people see the best, they'll still be embracing.

Part of our problem these days is not just the indifference that displaces compassion but the cold manipulation that's displacing intimacy. The relative collapse of families in America, especially in black America, means that the very act of intimacy is being destroyed.

◆

When I was growing up, we were targeted for love and people cared for us. They were concerned about us. Folk in the church would give you generous portions of wisdom, most often unsolicited. Folk in the Little League or in the beauty salon just kept dropping all these different pearls that you didn't even realize were wisdom until you strung them together in a moment of crisis.

Young brothers and sisters today have no sense of the signs, signals, clues, and cues needed to negotiate and navigate the treacherous terrain of American society.

It's not just how you dress. It's in language, nuance, tone, judgment, and timing, all those things you learn in your family. You don't learn them in a book. You have to learn them by spending time around other folk who've had to negotiate and navigate on that same terrain for a long time. That's partly what I mean by the young folk not being loved right and not getting enough care and attention.

◆

Historically for so many, but especially for black people, the church has been an extended family. The church gave you a sense of history, memory, and the need for struggle. The church at its best was the upholder of truth, love, and justice.

◆

We live in a society that suffers from historical amnesia. We find it very difficult to preserve the memory of those who have resisted and struggled for the ideals of freedom, democracy, and equality.

That's why young people need to read their history closely. To prepare themselves spiritually for struggle. To be self-critical and open to counsel from elders who have been engaged in purposeful struggle their entire lives.

Young people need hope. They need to hold on to the notion that the future can be different—if they sacrifice, if they fight, if they struggle.

◆

I try to uplift young people by introducing them to historic individuals who have displayed courage in its highest form—people like Dr. Martin Luther King, Jr., Rabbi Abraham Joshua Heschel, Michael Harrington, Ida B. Wells-Barnett, and other freedom fighters. Then I ask them how many of their parents and brothers and sisters in some way extend this kind of tradition. I ask them: What's going to happen to this tradition? Are you going to be part of this tradition? How can we keep it vital, vibrant, and alive?

Parenting is the
ultimate nonmarket activity
in a market-driven society.

We need to make sure parents are spiritually, politically, and economically nourished enough to be able to parent young people.

◆

In parenting, we've socialized the benefits and privatized the costs. If you do good parenting, you sacrifice and society benefits. Yet society doesn't help you very much.

If young people don't turn out that well and end up in jail, society pays the cost of the prison-industrial complex: billions of dollars, destroyed communities, and wasted lives.

◆

Parenting itself is pushed to the margins, mostly by means of mass media. Today parents are breaking their necks trying to have some influence on their kids. They're working and the TV is on all the time when they're away.

Young people often conform to what they see on TV, and to what the media feeds them. You end up with the young and fashionable being shaped by the marketplace.

Look at the lives of our young people—rich, middle class or poor. There's a vast desert of sadness in their souls.

Without direct intervention and commitment, they're still the future of our nation. It's a very troubling affair.

◆

In the modern era, we've allowed our children's souls to grow emptier, our schools have become a disgrace, and our communities have been shattered. Fathers can't get jobs, mothers are overworked and underpaid, and everyone is longing for real intimacy. And our young people are left dangling. It just gets worse and worse, generation after generation.

Then sooner or later, someone says, "We're in a state of emergency!" No, you've been in it for a long time. You just refused to acknowledge it.

◆

Older black folk have seen so many efforts come to naught and they're just trying to survive. But young folk still have a sense of spring. I call it *spring consciousness*—a consciousness full of dreams and possibilities, and a willingness to sacrifice.

To bloom in spring, young people must read history closely. They must prepare themselves spiritually for struggle. They must become self-critical and be open to counsel from older freedom fighters.

◆

How can the malaise that so much of black America finds itself in be resolved? When we look around the black community we see prophetic churches and mosques, and although many of them are deeply flawed, they nevertheless remain linked to the black freedom struggle.

This struggle still produces people who exude and exemplify prophetic values that they exalt and extol in their daily lives. We see political organizations, neighborhood block associations, Big Brother/Big Sister programs, and sports leagues. Although these community-sponsored activities might seem minuscule, they are actually critical character-building activities that can inspire young people to engage in the struggle.

◆

Professor William Julius Wilson's claim that middle class flight helped create the social disintegration of the black underclass is only half the story. He is correct that there is a disconnect between the black middle class and the black poor. However, economically, the black middle class had nothing to do with the history of joblessness and unemployment facing the black underclass. That's part of the larger structural and economic problems of America, which the black middle class, who are primarily white collar workers, has no control over—a point Wilson makes but we often forget!

It's unreasonable to expect the black middle class, which is fragile economically, and highly anxiety-ridden psychologically, to save the race. In fact, it just creates more guilt and anxiety to maintain that they have both the capacity and the responsibility to save the black poor.

The middle class does have a responsibility to enhance the conditions of the black poor by means of structures and institutions—black churches, fraternities, etc., but they alone don't have the capacity to do it. We do have some upper class individuals who have a moral responsibility to our community, but even they can't be responsible for elevating the black underclass all by themselves. Only economic justice across the board—like a Marshall Plan for the poor—can elevate the underclass.

◆

Today, even our black colleges have become deeply shaped by capitalist values. Most of our students are graduating in business and communication, and find humanistic studies decorative.

"Oh, that's something I have to take because it's part of a path that the old folk used to study but I want to make that money! I'm going to zip through this humanities class to take my business class because I'm gonna be rich."

That's not just the aspiration of black students, that's students across the board. This bling bling attitude is deeply shaping the values of a whole new generation to whom Malcolm X is Malcolm the Tenth, and Martin Luther King, Jr. is some cultural icon that has no connection whatsoever to their everyday lives. What a challenge!

◆

We have a generation that is the most schooled in the history of black people, but in a deep sense they're still not the most educated. Their attention is "for sale" to the highest bidder. Mindless repetition is what pleasure, instant gratification and addiction are all about. Indiscriminate consumption and distraction is the twirling of a top that just goes around and around.

If you start from bling bling, g-string, egoism, narcissism, and hedonism, and someone asks you to shift your attention toward truth, justice, compassion, and service—it can be difficult to comprehend initially but that's what education in its deepest sense is—the turning of the soul.

◆

The aim of education is to get people to shift from the surface to something substantive. You can have all the schooling in the world, but if you're still on the surface, you're not really educated. You can't engage in that turning of the soul without history, memory, and wrestling with mortality so that your soul becomes mature.

So, you end up with the most brilliant young people whose souls are underdeveloped because they haven't been educated in that sense. They are twirling tops. They're brilliant, exposed to the world, can talk about Europe, Africa, and Asia, and know six or seven languages, which is beautiful and impressive. It's a nice skill that the system can use, but in terms of *deep education,* the education of the soul, it's not sufficient.

To be truly educated, you need a sense of history and the courage to examine yourself and the world, but you also need examples. You have to have direct access to examples. Good examples are the go-cart of good judgments.

◆

We often have nostalgic thoughts about the older people in our lives who really affected us. This could be grandmothers, aunts, uncles, the old sister down the street, or the brother hanging out in front of the store. We remember how their concrete examples stirred our souls because we had real access to them.

◆

You can't gain access to wise judgment just through schooling. "Schooling" means you follow the rules, do well on the tests, and say what the boss wants you to say for a promotion. Judgment comes from both a cultivated mind and intelligence, but also from hanging around people who are grand examples of greatness and who exercise wise judgment. If you don't have those kinds of people in your life, you're not going to be moved enough to really want to know what deep education is.

◆

In the culture we live in, families don't even eat together, so there's not much interaction. The older generation watches one TV show and the younger is looking at another. One generation listens to one kind of music, the other generation listens to another kind of music.

The number of deep conversations that a young person actually has with somebody who is 65 years old are few and far between. They're never exposed to our most valuable examples.

They're hungry for this kind of exposure and look for it in celebrities. **Instead of talking with granddad they go to the media or their peers.**

The crucial element that goes into deep education is access to grand examples of greatness so that one learns how to make wise and great judgments, and thereby live a wise and great life. **Deep education requires a habitual vision of greatness.**

◆

When we're talking about education, it can't just be classroom schooling, as important as that is. We need to think also of the education that takes place in family and communities. Think, for example, of author James Baldwin, and the brilliant artist who mentored him. Baldwin said, "There is no me without Beauford Delaney." His stepfather in Harlem hated and abused him. His mother loved him, but she was locked in the family life in Harlem. Delaney came along and literally saved Baldwin's life.

Malcolm X was the same way. He was a gangster in a cell until the Honorable Elijah Muhammad loved him and turned his soul from bling and g-string in the streets of Detroit, New

York, and Boston to self-love and love of black people. Then Malcolm began to even love white folk and others, which was something Elijah couldn't fully get to.

Consider the concrete example of Malcolm X. In the beginning, he was just a young, Negro gangster. In the end, he was a courageous freedom fighter and rhetorical genius. Without the safety net of extended family, black folk would be lost.

◆

Relationships are an essential part of family life—whether it's our immediate relationships or relationships in our extended family. Sisters have to talk to brothers. They have to love us enough to tell us the truth about ourselves. So when we start acting up and acting pathetic, we need to be held accountable. But it's got to be informed by love. So when Mom tells me something, I don't mind the correction if the compassion is there. And the same is true of our relationship to sisters. So I think sisters ought to be harsh in a loving way, because we need some serious correction.

◆

We're not going to get out of our current societal mess unless we engage the younger generation. Our young folk are out there and they're struggling. They've got unbelievable creativity and imagination, and they are trying to channel their moral outrage.

In some sense, they're imitating us—our materialism, careerism, and so on—but in another sense, they also have grown up in a different kind of world. Their world is so market-saturated that it's hard for them to gain access to non-buying-and-selling values and activities that they can give weight to because everybody's saying, "Gimme, gimme, gimme!"

◆

On one hand, young people, and black and brown youth in particular, are disengaged and alienated from the political system. On the other hand, they have this incredible hunger and thirst for something better.

Young people in black America, at their best, are the vanguard in the quest for self-love and self-regard and self-respect.

They are responding to broken communities and constrained opportunities. They are falling back on the traditions forged by black families and communities in the fire of oppression that have helped black folk stay sane.

Singing through the storm
                    has helped us sustain
            our sense of self,
                    our sense of family,
        and our sense of community.

© Cornel West

CHAPTER SEVEN

MUSIC

> You can't create art
>   without courage, discipline,
> and being tied to a tradition.

The black musical tradition is unique in this country because
it assumes, without question, the full humanity of Americans

of African descent, and thereby allows blacks and others to revel in it.

◆

It was music that sustained Africans on the slave ships making their way from Africa to the New World. We often didn't speak a common language that allowed us to communicate with each other in a deep way. We had to constitute some form of comradery and community, and music did that. It preserved our sanity, as well as our dignity.

When you look at this tradition from the spirituals on through Louis Armstrong, Sarah Vaughan, Curtis Mayfield, Luther Vandross, and Aretha Franklin on up to Prince and Gerald Levert, music sustained our humanity, dignity, and integrity.

◆

Owing to white supremacist sanctions, enslaved Africans were not allowed to read or write. As a nonliterate people, we learned to manifest our genius through what no one could take away— our voices and our music.

> We come from a tradition
>   where the musicians are supreme—
> there are 10 works of musical genius
>   for every one work of literary genius.

Our literary giants view themselves in many ways as intellectual literary extensions of those great musical geniuses. It's no accident that our greatest writer, Toni Morrison, has often said that she would like to write the way Sarah Vaughan sings. And did not Ralph Ellison try to write like Louis Armstrong blew his horn?

◆

Black preaching is inseparable from black singing. Most secular black singers come out of the choir, and the lives of the congregation hang on how they sing the song, what they put into the song, how passionate, how self-invested they are. Preaching is just less visible to the outside world as an art form because words uttered once don't have the same status as cultural products, but the black preachers are artists with a very long tradition.

Tremendous gravity and weight are given to these artistic church performances because people's lives hang on them. They provide some hope from week to week so that these folk won't fall into hopelessness and meaninglessness, so they won't kill themselves. The responsibility of the black preacher-artist is, in that sense, deeply functional, but at the same time it requires a refinement of a form bequeathed to him by our ancestors.

◆

Think about traditional opera in the West. Let's go back to Richard Strauss's *Capriccio* in 1942. It was in some ways the last great classical opera.

In the last scene, they're wrestling over the ancient quarrel between philosophy and poetry. Strauss recasts the question and asks, "What is greater, poetry or instrumental music?"

They have this big scene in D-major. There is a huge mirror. The woman looks in the mirror and sees herself. Instead of choosing one or the other, she says, "The human voice is the greatest!"

The human voice itself is the greatest instrument. Black folks' tradition begins with the voice. We try to make the instruments sound like our voices. Art Tatum vocalizes the piano. John Coltrane vocalizes the saxophone. Miles Davis vocalizes the trumpet. It's the human voice you hear in the instrument. The human voice goes beyond technology, the poetry of the written page, and instrumental music.

◆

The irony is that you can't find your voice unless you're bouncing off the voices of the dead. That's where tradition plays a role. Everybody knows that Jelly Roll Morton is gone. Buddy Bolden is gone. But their voices are still here.

There's no Wynton Marsalis without Duke Ellington. Duke is the voice of the dead. Now Wynton is in deep conversation. He's in relation so he can create by finding his own voice. He is relating to someone who has expressed his voice in such a profound way. You get this wonderful interplay between past and present, which creates a new future musically.

◆

Music has been our most powerful creative expression. Of course, the music itself is based on the communal links of church, family, and social education. Our music reflects our unique sense of rhythm, harmony, and melody.

◆

For me, the deepest existential source of coming to terms with white racism is music. In some ways, this is true for black America as a whole, from spirituals and blues through jazz, rhythm and blues, and even up to hip-hop.

From the very beginning, **I always conceived of myself as an aspiring bluesman in a world of ideas and a jazzman in the life of the mind.** What is distinctive about using blues and jazz as a source of intellectual inspiration is the ability to be flexible, fluid, improvisational, and multi-dimensional—finding one's own voice, but using that voice in a variety of different ways.

◆

The motif for my work has always been to sing in spoken word and written texts like Duke Ellington played and Sarah Vaughan sang, to swing, to create an intellectual performance that has a blues sensibility and jazzlike openness, to have the courage to be myself and find my voice in the world of ideas and in the life of the academy.

◆

When we first encountered white brothers and sisters in junior high school, and we saw the way they walked, danced, and talked, that was the last thing we wanted in life.

They thought the Beach Boys were so sharp. We were bringing in Smokey Robinson and James Brown, Dyke and the Blazers. They all wanted to be like us. They acknowledged it. "This is some happening stuff. Our stuff is flatfooted." They affirmed our cultural excellence based on the quality of the music and style. I've always felt that. I believe that today.

◆

If you're going to understand what's going on in American culture, you must come to terms with popular culture. When I talk about Sarah Vaughan, and I could talk about Kenneth "Babyface" Edmonds, or Marvin Gaye, or a host of others,

I'm not just talking about some ornamental or decorative cultural celebrity. I'm talking about people who kept me alive.

James Brown makes a difference in my life.
That's a fact.

American musical heritage rests, in large part, on the artistic genius of black composers and performers.

This rich tradition of black music is not only an artistic response to the psychic wounds and social scars of a despised people. More importantly, it enacts in dramatic forms the creativity, dignity, grace, and elegance of African Americans without wallowing in self-pity or wading in white put-down.

◆

Any time you shatter innocence and find yourself wrestling with deep experiences of suffering, grief, and sorrow, you will find yourself working in the raw stuff of great art.

> Blues is not about
> optimism.
> Nor is it about pessimism.
> It is about hope.

Blues sensibility is tragicomic but not sentimental. There are no pure heroes or impure victims. Good and evil are locked in all our souls. The question is, what kind of *choices* do we want to make?

◆

Robert Johnson found his voice through the guitar. It's not the old guitar versus the electric guitar. It's: Are you vocalizing whatever instrument you have?

Bob Dylan is a white blues brother from Minnesota, but he isn't Robert Johnson. Bruce Springsteen is another great white blues brother. He isn't Muddy Waters either. He knows that. He appreciates it. He is a genius in his own way. There is the importance of knowing from whence you came.

◆

What is jazz all about? It's about finding your voice. It's about that long, difficult walk to freedom. It's about mustering the courage to think critically. **It's about mustering the courage to care and love, and be empathetic and compassionate.**

But it's also about being in a group with antagonistic cooperation, which means bouncing against one another so that you're giving each other more and more courage to engage in higher levels of collective performance.

Jazz is a mode of democratic action, just as blues is a mode of deep, tear-soaked individuality.

Charlie Parker didn't give a damn. Jazz is the middle road between invisibility and anger. It is where self-confident creativity resides. Black music is the paradigm for how black people have best dealt with their humanity, their complexity, their good and bad, negative and positive aspects, without being excessively preoccupied with whites. Duke Ellington, Louis Armstrong, and Coltrane were just being themselves. And for whites interested in the humanity of the "other," jazz—a purely American form—provides them with examples of sheer and rare genius.

◆

What Parker did, of course, was to Africanize jazz radically: to accent the polyrhythms, to combine these rhythms with unprecedented virtuosity on the sax. He said explicitly that his music was not produced to be accepted by white Americans. He would be suspicious if it were.

◆

One of the reasons jazz is so appealing to large numbers of white Americans is precisely because they feel that in this black musical tradition, not just black musicians, but black humanity is being asserted by artists who do not look at themselves in relation to whites or engage in self-pity or white put-down. This type of active, as opposed to reactive, expression is very rare in any aspect of African American culture.

◆

Louis Armstrong was an existential democrat, which meant that he believed in the dignity of ordinary people, and the potentiality of everyday people.

If you have enough courage to lift your voice, become an agent in the world connecting with other voices, you can democratize your situation—because democracy is about voice lifting, and lack of democracy is about lack of voice.

In performance, it's your body as part of your voice, your critical intelligence as part of your voice, your feelings and passions as part of your voice. It's a matter of mind, body, and soul.

◆

In the 60s there was the brilliance of Berry Gordy's Motown, with great talents like Marvin Gaye, Stevie Wonder, Gladys Knight, Diana Ross, and Mary Wells. Kenneth Gamble and Leon Huff's Philly Sounds followed with artists such as The Intruders, The O'Jays, The Spinners, and Teddy Pendergrass. And who could surpass the two giants of this new moment, James Brown and Aretha Franklin? They solidified this monumental shift in black music. There's no doubt about that.

Popular music had political implications that created an openness. It became one of the major means that allowed us to be in direct contact with each other's humanity, even while racist public institutions and practices were at work.

◆

Blues and jazz lost much of their black audience in the 50s and 60s when they abandoned black public spaces, such as black dances, clubs, and street corners. Without access to the participatory rituals in public spaces of black everyday life, blues and jazz became marginal to ordinary working black people in urban centers. In their stead, rhythm and blues, soul music, and now hip-hop seized the imagination and pocketbook of young black America.

This fundamental shift in the musical tastes of black America resulted from two basic features of the larger American culture industry: the profit-driven need to increase the production pace and number of records, reinforcing fashion, fad, and novelty, and the explosive growth of black talent spilling out of churches and clubs in search of upward social mobility. The lessening of racist barriers in the industry and wider acceptance of black music by white consumers created new opportunities. Since neither blues nor jazz could satisfy or saturate this market, they fell by the cultural wayside or, at least, were pushed to the margins.

◆

It is no surprise that black hits last a shorter time than white hits on the bestseller charts: the selective black audience expects more. Is not amateur night every Wednesday at the Apollo Theater in Harlem one of the most aesthetically discriminating and democratic moments in American culture? **The pop music industry looks more and more like the National Basketball Association:** a rapid succession of outstanding young black talent hustling to survive against the constant onrush of new competition in an oversaturated market.

◆

Hip-hop music is the most important popular musical development in the last thirty years. It is a profound extension of the improvisational character of what I call the Afro-American spiritual blues impulse, which is an attempt to hold the demons and devils at bay. Hip-hop allows a kind of marriage between the rhetorical and the musical by means of some of the most amazing linguistic virtuosity we have seen in the English language. Just listen to the lyrical genius of Rakim, Snoop Dogg, or Jay-Z.

At their best, these artists respond to their sense of being rejected by society at large, of being invisible in the society at large, with a subversive critique of that society. It has to do with both the description and depiction of the conditions under which they're forced to live, as well as a description and depiction of the humanity preserved by those living in such excruciating conditions. It then goes beyond to a larger critique of the power structure as a whole.

◆

I was just reading a Jay-Z interview. He said, *I wanted to get out of the Marcy projects. First, I wanted to make money. Then when I made money, I wanted to make history. I couldn't make money or history unless I prepared myself. I had to hang out with the best, which was Biggie.*

Jay-Z came to my class at Princeton. I had just given a lecture on Plato and Socrates. He said, "All my life I've always wanted to play

"You *can't* **lead** the people if you *don't love* the people."

"You *can't save* the people if you *don't serve* the people."

Plato to Biggie's Socrates." Plato worked his whole life to keep alive the legacy and memory of Socrates so the world would never forget there was a man named Socrates. He said, "That's what I'm going to do with Biggie." It's that kind of passion that leads to preparation.

Shakespeare says, "Ripeness is all." Readiness is all. **You become ripe and ready by preparing through tremendous discipline.** That's what you actually get in the written works of Richard Wright, Ralph Ellison, and James Baldwin. They were just assiduously preparing themselves. They were reading all the time and talking to people who read. They were reflecting and exploring a sense of adventure. They were taking risks. They were willing to be pushed in the danger zone intellectually and existentially.

The best of the hip-hop world is like that. That's why I read all these hip-hop magazines. I read every page, because I'm concerned with how every young person is trying to escape misery, death, and pain. They throw themselves into it wholeheartedly. They spend 10 to 12 hours a day coming up with verses. It's unbelievable.

Yet, too many young folk can't even play instruments. They don't understand how towering geniuses like Stevie Wonder or Prince—who played every instrument on all 30 albums—reached their heights. It took discipline, concentration, genius, sacrifice, deferred gratification, a deep sense of calling, and a love of music. This is what I love about Lil Wayne—his incredible love for and dedication to his craft.

◆

Too often, hip-hop still lacks deep vision and analysis. It's just escapism, it's thin. It's too morally underdeveloped and spiritually immature. In the end, it can't just be about escaping. It has to be more of a turning-to in order to constructively contribute.

It's fun, it's entertaining, it helps sustain the rituals of party-going on the weekends, but it still lacks a deep vision. Thank God for KRS-One!

◆

The recording industry is so interested in pacifying, distracting, and ensuring that the strength, grace, and dignity of young people is not affirmed. They would rather keep them locked into a narcissistic, materialistic, and individualist orientation.

When you market disposable bubblegum music, you're going to get some disposable dispositions toward each other.

In 150 or 200 years from now, people will say, "What were intellectuals doing with regard to black music?"

Black music will remain an attempt by certain highly talented cultural artists to socialize generations in light of the success or failure of our civil society.

◆

There is the importance of knowing from whence you came. It's hard for a lot of young people to acknowledge the degree to which the way they walk, talk, and sing are all products of historical memory.

◆

If they had a chance to be in conversation with the voices of the dead, they would hear their own voices. They would recognize, "I can't move forward until I move backward. There were earlier creations that paved the way for my own sense of who I am, how I speak, and so forth." This is what Sankofa is all about— going back to the roots to move forward in our routes!

◆

A rich heritage wanes when a great tradition fails to inspire and instruct young artists whose creativity is based, in part, on a sense of the past. Artists thrive best when they're not simply producers of objects of private consumption but also participants in the everyday public rituals of the larger culture. The challenge artists face today is whether to be an underground, unheard genius, or to dilute their art for the marketplace.

Young black America may hold the key to reaching such a golden mean. The powerful forces of the marketplace cannot be expected to yield a new generation of young black people in touch with their musical tradition. In the black America of the future, the crucial pillars of our musical heritage are threatening to crumble. Yet our young musical geniuses, standing on the shoulders of those who have come before, still have the potential to turn the tide.

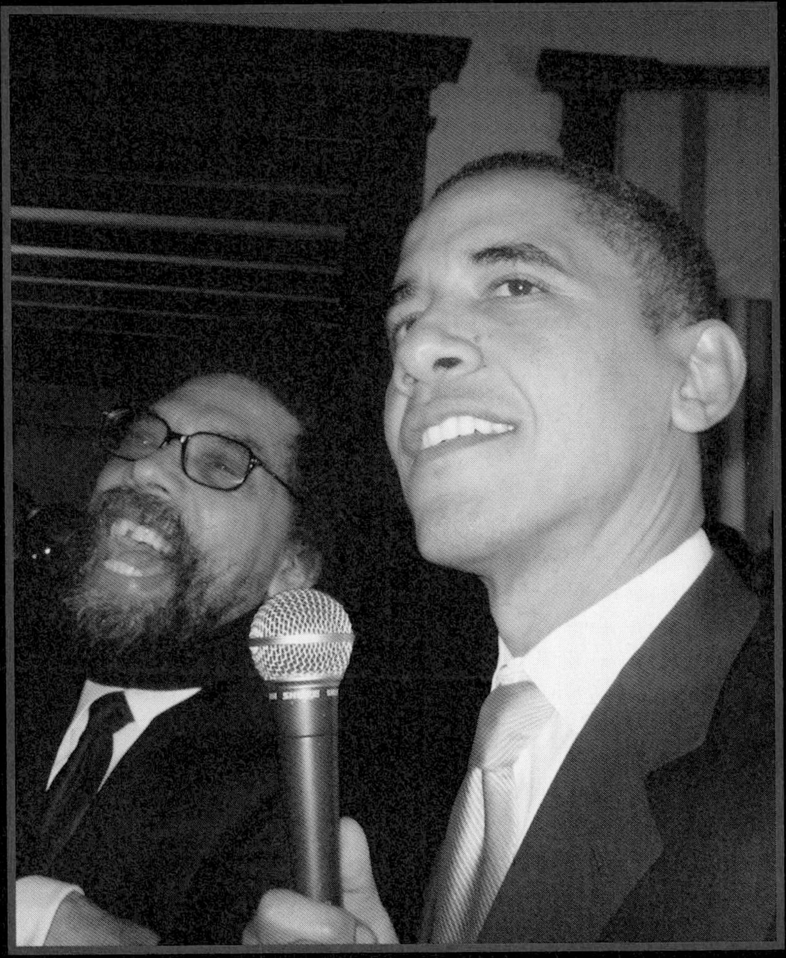

© Fredrica S. Goodman

CHAPTER EIGHT

LEADERSHIP

Visionary leadership is predicated
on a leap of faith and a labor of love.

Leadership is fundamental because there can be no significant social movement without visionary and analytical leadership by people of courage and integrity. We are not talking about one person, we're talking about a conscious collective.

◆

It is a deeply democratic ideal that says that ordinary people ought to be able to lead, that "the people" ought to be able to participate in the decision-making process of the institutions that guide and regulate their lives.

◆

Luminaries don't come down from heaven. Leaders come out of their momma's womb, like all of us, and at some point, they'll go to their graves.

◆

Once you view yourself as, first and foremost, an isolated individual, you're not going to be able to summon the courage required to sustain leadership. Nobody has that kind of capacity. Even Jesus needed disciples. He needed his friends even when he knew they were cowardly and would betray him.

◆

When you look at the world through the lens of the cross, you have to be willing to pick up your own cross. Every cross leaves its marks, wounds, and scars. In the end, you may have to die on that cross. Therefore, we need leaders who dare to have that kind of cross-centeredness.

To be a
great leader,
you must
habitually envision
greatness.

Towering black leaders like Frederick Douglass, Ida B. Wells-Barnett, Martin Luther King, Jr., and Fannie Lou Hamer had a tremendous sense of mission. They were rooted in courage and a profound commitment to love, serve, and lead black people.

These legends also had a deep sense of history. They understood that they were part of a tradition. They found the very meaning of life in giving to others. To them **the present was history in the making. It wasn't something located in a museum.** History was a vital, vibrant process that they believed they could help write.

◆

Throughout American history there were forestalled moments when great black leaders could have been killed by American terrorists, or wiped off the face of the earth by cowardly white supremacists. The result? We wouldn't have had the kind of leadership necessary for America to mature and overcome its ignorance and crimes against black people.

◆

Leading blacks versus *black leaders* are two different species identified by my dear Sister, Dr. Julia Hare. Leading black faces in high places are comforting representatives for a white audience. For the most part, they have been try-ing to speak to and soothe white fears, insecurities, and anxieties.

Black leaders are those who love black people enough to tell them the truth, respect them enough to believe that they can wrestle with the truth, and are willing to sacrifice enough to pay some serious costs. Leading blacks don't want to take such risks and aren't willing to bear those costs.

They are content to sit in those high places and be rep-resentative of "great progress," part of a more colorful glass menagerie in corporate America.

◆

There's a growing cowardice in the black community. Too many leading blacks are afraid to lead. They want to get in on the goodies and grab the booty of the empire. We're seeing it more and more.

◆

We must never forget that the pressures on bold black leaders are so immense and intense that without spiritual strength and candid friends who challenge you with love, one cannot but give up, cave in, or sell out. The temptations and seductions of the status quo are always waiting.

◆

Our leaders need to understand that eliminating poverty is not just in the interest of poor people. Eliminating poverty means you might be able to walk the streets with ease, you might be able to produce a quality labor force, you might even be able to cut back on the expansion of the prison-industrial complex. It means you might even be able to envision and experience quality relationships between black and white leaders.

◆

Today's leaders are too often part of a process of compromise that makes it impossible to speak with boldness and defiance about the realities that people are facing.

© Kawai Matthews

Achieving high office—to be a mayor or governor or a state legislator, that's fine, but it puts you on a different track. Mainstream elected leaders can be progressive on the inside but their prophetic juices can't flow very easily. Until recently, black folk have rarely had leaders on the inside. But when black political leaders get on the inside, too often we discover they're like any other politician. They're concerned about the next election, their patronage system, and maintaining their constituency. Why should we expect any different?

◆

You can't develop and sustain black leaders unless you get motion and momentum on the ground among ordinary people. There's no way that you can rally the spiritual strength and the willingness to sacrifice unless you're part of a grassroots movement in the community.

◆

The leadership of the black church must change to meet new challenges. It must become more sophisticated, critical, and self-critical. This is the only way that it can become more relevant and persuasive in the black community. Black church leadership must become more grounded in intellectual inquiry as well. No longer can we have leaders who simply engage in moral condemnation and ethical rhetoric. The black church must understand—and help others understand—how power and wealth operate in this society.

◆

It is no accident that Malcolm X now comes back not solely as an icon but as a great leader for many conscious young black people. Today, Malcolm X, the major articulator of black rage in the civil rights era, is resurrected as a great leader. What's different about Malcolm X from Elijah Muhammad, Fannie Lou Hamer, or Martin Luther King, Jr., is that Malcolm X was never able to establish his own organization to direct his rage.

It was only when he was with Elijah and the Nation of Islam that his rage was directed. When he broke from Elijah the rage overflowed and the conservative forces in American society were just waiting to express their contempt and hatred for black people. The Watts riots in 1965, and the Detroit and Newark uprisings in 1967, reflected the growing political consciousness in black America, yet these eruptions of black rage had little organization or direction.

◆

Without leadership, black rage will remain chaotic and ultimately self-destructive. Consider the Rodney King riots in 1992, the lives lost, and the estimated one billion dollars in damage. When black rage is channeled by leaders of integrity into relevant organizations, change will become contagious throughout our society.

◆

There is human potential for outrage in all of us, no matter what color we are. The tradition of oppression and repression from slavery to "driving while black" deeply shaped black consciousness in America. Don't tell black people who are upset and full of anger, rage, and righteous indignation that somehow they're just angry at white folk in the abstract. That's a lie! We can separate John Brown from his cousins.

◆

Obama says Jeremiah Wright is angry because he's part of an older generation. That's not true. Walk the streets of Brooklyn. The young brothers and sisters are angry and full of rage right now. Katrina was just three years ago. You and I are still full of righteous indignation. We didn't need to grow up under Jim Crow to be like Bigger Thomas in terms of the rage simmering inside.

The question is, How do you express your righteous indignation? The assumption and the dominant white perspective is that, if you have an angry Negro, that Negro's anger is somehow unjust. That's inaccurate. You can have rage against injustice and still recognize that not all white folk are complicit.

◆

Elijah Muhammad and Martin Luther King, Jr., understood one fundamental truth about black rage: it must be neither ignored nor ignited. This is what separates them from the great Malcolm X. Malcolm articulated black rage in a manner unprecedented in American history, yet his broad black nationalist platforms were too vague to give this black rage any concrete direction. Elijah and Martin knew how to work with black rage in a constructive manner: they shaped it through moral discipline, channeled it into political organization, and guided it by visionary leadership.

Black rage is as American as apple pie. This is why the future of our cities, states, and nation depend on whether we will acknowledge legitimate black rage, how we will respond to it, and if bold and wise leaders will direct it.

◆

Young people need to know that, in the 60s, Eugene Redmond, Amiri Baraka, Haki Madhubuti, Sonia Sanchez, and others loved black people enough to turn a spotlight on black suffering and affirm that black people counted. So much so that their writings became a form of political action and bearing witness.

Young folk are disconnected from that history of sacrifice and commitment. They wonder how much we really love them. They've been told that "We shall overcome" means going to some dynamite college, getting some magnificent skill, and living large in some vanilla suburb. That's American success. It's part of the story. But that's just *part* of the story.

◆

There's no doubt that Barack Obama and his campaign constitute an unprecedented historical phenomenon in the past and present of America. It shows the degree to which the vicious legacy of white supremacy has been punctured in regard to perception and black faces in high places.

At the same time, his success is contrasted against tremendous suffering in chocolate cities and urban areas where a disproportionate amount of black and poor people live. You get this fascinating juxtaposition of real access to the White House and actually having a black man as the public face of the American Empire trying to regenerate democratic possibilities. On the other hand, black, white, brown, red, and yellow poor are still suffering.

◆

I'd like to see my dear Brother Barack Obama in the White House. I think he's the best presidential candidate. At the same time, there are structural constraints on any president.

Any politician who makes it to the level of a Barack Obama, Hillary Clinton, or anybody else tends to be surrounded by spin-meisters and pundits who do not put the suffering of working and poor people at the center of their vision.

◆

I want Senator Obama to win, but I'm going to criticize him intensely when he wins. I'm a deep democrat and he's a liberal. They're not the same thing. I very much support him, but it's a question of principle. The plight of everyday people is paramount.

When our local and national leadership is indifferent to the underclass, we all pay the bill. For all we know, the next Martin Luther King, Jr., or Frederick Douglass or Ida B. Wells-Barnett could have been in the black underclass and snuffed out. We don't know if our indifference has destroyed the next great black leader. It's hard to say. That's just how precarious our experiment in democracy is.

◆

Brother Jay-Z is from the Marcy Projects in Brooklyn. I visited his place in Manhattan. I had tears in my eyes because I know where he comes from. I know his lyrical genius. At the same time I asked the brother, "You are successful now, but are you great?" That's something else.

"You come from a people whose greatness has a quality of service and depth of love toward others. These are the criteria for greatness. I can revel in your success, but can I celebrate your greatness?"

Today, Jay-Z is one of America's most pioneering and successful hip-hop artist-entrepreneurs, as well as a new wave philanthropist—taking on the global water shortage.

I believe that Jay-Z is both successful and great.

◆

If we present cowardly, complacent, or narrowly successful examples as great examples, that's the kind of leadership we're going to get. Young folk are shaped by what older folk present to them. If young folk have access to a vast array of courageous and great examples, that will serve as the foundation for their judgment.

Examples are the go-cart of judgment. Bad examples, bad judgments. Great examples, great judgments. Who are the examples? Jesus, Muhammad, Martin, Gandhi, Mandela, my father, your mother, my mother—people of all colors. Let's keep the focus on their actions and behaviors. Consider the example of George Bush. He never used the *n* word, but look at his example and judgment with Katrina. His action—or lack of action—was based on bad judgment. Bush helped niggerize us without ever using the *n* word!

◆

We must pray that our next generation of leaders aren't destroyed before they have a chance to arrive. We have to remember that if it'd been up to black leaders, Martin would never have surfaced.

◆

Black politicians rarely mention the prison-industrial complex. We have entire presidential campaigns that never mentioned this reality. There's talk about the connection between the criminal justice system and the prison-industrial complex because everyone's agreed to be *hard on crime*. And hard on crime means *war*—against our poor and disproportionately black young people.

◆

With over two million American men in jail, 41 percent black, 37 percent non-Hispanic white, and 19 percent Hispanic, what will it take for the black community to challenge the new business-as-usual? How many of our children need to be in prison before we get indignant? Unless you think our children are genetically inferior and somehow deserve their fate. White supremacy dies a very slow, pseudoscientific death.

◆

We need a new kind of black leadership, new kinds of black organizations and associations that can bring power and pressure to bear on the powers that be. One cannot talk about enhancing the plight of the black underclass without talking about politics, and to talk about politics is to talk about mobilization and organization.

◆

There can be no fundamental social change in the United States without creating cleavages and conflict among the power elite. They are not a monolithic group. And the degree to which they're in conflict and unable to reach consensus is the degree to which new possibilities will advance for those below.

◆

Including black women in positions of leadership is not a moral luxury. It is a necessity. You can't have an oppressed community depending on 48 percent of its resources. You need 100 percent of all of your talent.

Black women are going to be the crucial part of the next wave of our collective leadership.

CHAPTER NINE

LOVE AND SERVICE

Y ou can't lead the people if you don't love the people. You can't save the people if you don't serve the people.

◆

I want to know: How deep is your love for the people? What kind of courage have you demonstrated in the stances that you've taken? What are you willing to sacrifice for? These are the fundamental questions. I don't care what color you are.

◆

James Baldwin talked about love explicitly as the most difficult, dangerous, but also the most significant force in the world. Why? Because if you come from a people who have been so hated, love can become subversive and transformative. You must begin by loving yourself.

◆

We choose to be certain kinds of human beings. That is why those who choose to love and serve have a calling and not a career. Love and service are a vocation, not a profession.

◆

Christians are a rich footnote to prophetic Judaism. For us to be human is to practice a certain kind of loving-kindness or steadfast love that spotlights the most vulnerable or the least of these.

◆

I actually believe that loving your neighbor as yourself is a desirable way of being in the world, even though it may seem absurd given the kind of world we live in.

◆

For me, as a Christian, he or she who is greatest among us will be your servant. You must be willing to examine the quality of your service to others. Do you find joy in your service to others? **Do you actually believe that living is connected to giving?**

I can't wait to help others. Why? Because it's a beautiful thing—and because I know that you can never repay what your mother, father, grandmother, and grandfather did for you. If you're Christian, you will never be able to repay the price that Jesus paid on the cross. All of that blood, all of that love gushing out at the foot of the cross.

◆

There are too many children living in poverty, too many disgraceful school systems, and too much dilapidated housing in chocolate cities, too much childcare and healthcare that's unavailable. There is too much unemployment and underemployment, and not enough jobs with a living wage. Corporate greed is at the top, running amuck. Two percent of the population owns 51 percent of the wealth.

People are running around saying, "What would Jesus do?" The Roman Empire put him on a cross. How come? Because he was concerned with the least of these. He said all of us would be judged. Not on how sharp your clothes are, how long your car is, which neighborhood you live in, what ritual you undertook, or what ceremony you tried to perform.

What is the quality of your service, the depth of your love? What price are you willing to pay? What burden are you willing to bear? Be honest about it.

◆

Our Jewish brothers and sisters have this word, *hesed*, which is a steadfast love—". . . to act justly and to love mercy and to walk humbly with your God," Micah 6:8. That a Palestinian Jew named Jesus—who means everything to me—said, "Love your neighbor" in Matthew 5:43 and "Love your enemies" in Matthew 5:44—touches my soul.

Jesus's love talk took deep root and produced unbelievable flowers. His love fed the love talk of Martin Luther King, Jr., the love talk of John Coltrane's *Love Supreme*, and the love talk of Toni Morrison's *Beloved*. That is serious. Trying to keep alive this legacy of love for the younger generation is our responsibility. Our younger generation is too much unloved.

◆

I grew up in a neighborhood, not a 'hood. It was all black. Our neighborhood was a place where there were wonderful ties of sympathy and bonds of empathy. The folk who lived there kept track of you. A 'hood is survival of the slickest. They're obsessed with their 11th commandment, "Thou shalt not get caught." That's what young folk are up against.

That's why I have so much respect for young folk, even when I disagree with them. I don't know what it's like to grow up in a 'hood. I don't know what it's like to be unloved. I don't know what it's like to have a drifter for a father. I don't know what it's like to have my mother overworked and underpaid. I don't know what it's like to have to dodge bullets every time I go to class. I don't know what it's like to go to schools that don't even have textbooks.

I pay tribute to what they're wrestling with, even if I'm critical of the crack house, where too many of them end up. Even if I'm critical of the levels of disrespect, disregard, self-destruction and self-flagellation that we see too often in their relations with one another.

I say to myself, *We must take some responsibility. We should have taught them better how to care for and respect themselves. We should have taught them better how to love.*

◆

How can we as a people promote a renaissance of self-respect and self-love among black people, especially among young black people? When Brother Michael Eric Dyson and others say, *"Nigga* is really a term of endearment; it's really an expression of love." I say, "That's fine because it's all about the love, Brother. Because once we begin to love each other and love others, we've got something that's hard to stop because love is not some wayward sentiment. It's a steadfast commitment to the well-being of others."

◆

Martin Luther King, Jr., could use the *n* word all he wants—if he wanted to. Because he loved us enough to die for us. Malcolm could have used it. Elijah could have used it. Since I'm a Christian, I'm clear that we've also got to spill our love over into other communities. The essential thing is that we have to make love absolutely real.

◆

When you talk about Martin Luther King's love supreme, this is not just a hollow gesture or a clever sound bite. This profound love is rooted in a long tradition of struggle against institution-alized hatred that then became contagious, because other people wanted to be more human than they thought they were, too.

◆

You don't have a duty to complete this struggle, but neither are you free to desist from it, to cave in, or to give up. To love and serve is to persevere and endure.

◆

Malcolm X suggested, *Brother Martin, America has no soul. You're missing the point. It's about power.*

Martin replied, *I'm not naïve, Malcolm. I know a lot about power, but a democracy must also be about common good and public life, and I'm a democrat, small d.* And if you only play the game of power, then Thrasymachus is right in Plato's *Republic:* might makes right. I refuse to simply play the game of power, even though I bring power to bear with a moral vision.

As Malcolm continued to grow he realized, *You know, Martin, I'm beginning to see your point more clearly now. You're absolutely right. Even your language of love makes sense to me. Because it is, in fact, better to fight to save the soul rather than to blind oneself and live a soulless life in an imperial nation.*

It's a certain way of being in the world, a certain bearing witness. Even if you are unable to bring about the kind of changes you want in your generation, somebody will know ten years from now, twenty years from now, fifty years from now, that you bore witness. They will know that you dared to speak the truth and expose the lies so that you could bequeath that legacy to them.

◆

When we dare to love and serve, we will be willing to speak, act, dialogue, write, fuse, share, laugh, and love with others whom we can inspire and who can inspire us.

There's never any guarantee of victory in history. There never has been, there never will be. Nevertheless, if we can commit to loving, serving, and understanding each other—recognizing that we are far more alike than we are different—we have chance.

I pray that each one of you will dare to wrestle with these questions—about the quality of your love and the depth of your service to humanity.

◆

As we enter a period of economic downturn, many black communities are in a political, social, and economic state of siege. People are searching for black institutions that have some self-sufficiency. The black church has a critical role in helping to create more sustainable economic infrastructures in our community. We need prayer and access to economic resources for a variety of progressive purposes, from housing for the poor and elderly, to banks and credit unions, to advancing capital for black educational institutions and businesses. **We need a 21st-century-style love and service revival.**

◆

There are magnificent local activists whose commitment to unarmed truth and unconditional love has been quite extraordinary. You can go to different local communities and people can point them out, but today it is hard to find them at the national level.

◆

People are hungry for someone with the rare quality of a Martin Luther King. Jr. Someone who possesses the depth of his love, the quality of his service and his willingness to pursue unarmed truth and unconditional love. We must acknowledge that his mission was extraordinary because a Martin King does not come around every generation. Neither does a Fannie Lou Hamer.

Ella Baker used to say, "The movement made Martin" and it is true. He was unique and distinctive but the movement made him. Without that movement, you're not going to get the Martins and the Fannie Lous. It's very important to keep the historical context in mind as you contemplate the nature of love and service required in the 21st century.

◆

When you end up obsessed with success rather than greatness, prosperity rather that magnanimity, security rather than integrity—you end up with a generation of peacocks. Black peacocks walk around displaying their beautiful plumage. "Look at me. I'm so successful. I'm so accomplished. Look at my breakthroughs. I'm the first X, I'm the first Y, and I'm the first Z."

I can hear my grandmother saying from the back room, "Peacocks strut because they can't fly." I can hear her say, "You can't get off the ground. You are just a royal turkey, that's all you are."

Bling bling with no end and no aim is nothing but a form of idolatry. We've come out of a long tradition of service to others—not just blind obsession with the self.

◆

Love helps break down barriers, so even when black rage and righteous indignation have to look white supremacy in the face—in all of its dimensions that still persist—the language of love still allows black brothers and sisters to recognize that it's not all white people and it's not genetic.

White brothers and sisters can make choices. John Brown was part of the movement. Tom Hayden is part of the movement because it's all about choices, decisions, and commitments. No one is pushed into a pigeonhole or locked into a convenient category. That is why the ability to love and be loved in the highest sense is so crucial.

◆

The turning of the soul, the center of deep education, is created by deep love, care, and concern on behalf of another person who has been through hell and high water, and becomes a wise counselor. That's why the relationship between Malcolm and Elijah is so instructive. Without Elijah, Malcolm probably would have never made it. He would have remained just another Negro gangster and none of his potential would ever have been realized.

For Elijah to intervene in Malcolm's life when nobody else loved him was not just life transforming, it was a grand example of how black love can change the world. You cannot imagine black America without Malcolm. In some ways, you cannot imagine the world without him.

Even after his break with Elijah, Malcolm remained indebted. Even though he knew that Elijah had turned against him, he also knew that Elijah's love had transformed him.

We must have an unconditional commitment
to try to keep track of the humanity of each and every person
to give us the courage to love, serve, and sacrifice.

The worst thing in the world would be to be almost 60 years old and know you had a calling and you missed out on it. The soul was called but you didn't answer.

"I sounded like Nat King Cole and opted to play hockey. I'll be damned. All those folk who could have been touched by my singing in that silky soul voice will never know that joy. I settled for playing on the ice and I never really learned how to skate."

That's how you end up in the crack house. That's how alcohol gets you. It's understandable because you can't go back. You miss out. If Prince settled for being a janitor and violated his soul's call, his genius would never have been revealed.

Love what you do!
Do what you love!

CHAPTER TEN

SOCIAL JUSTICE

Brother Martin said a man can't ride your back unless it's bent. Nevertheless, it's hard to straighten your back because there's a price to be paid. What are the conditions under which black people will straighten their backs? *How do you shake the niggerization out of black people?*

When you examine the early stages of the niggerization of black people, we have to acknowledge the ways in which white supremacist practices became more and more predominant and systematized. I am talking about white greed, fear, and hatred extended so that black people became deeply traumatized and made to feel helpless and hopeless. We were denied the ability to love and affirm ourselves. Resisting or organizing against such oppression put our lives in jeopardy—as it still can today.

> The niggerization of black people
> tried to make black love a crime,
> black history a curse, black hope a joke,
> and black freedom a pipe dream.

You call Alexander "the Great." For what? He dominated more people than anyone in his day. You call Napoleon *great*. Why? He was conquering and killing. What happens if your criteria of greatness are not conquering and killing? What if the criteria are love, service, and social justice?

The West called Churchill *great*. He believed in the subhumanity of black people. He sided with Mussolini. Churchill was great in resisting Nazism for the British Empire, I grant him that. If you want to define greatness in that way, yes, he was a great man. But don't think that just because your suffering is at the center of your discussion that you can discount mine.

Is Minister Louis Farrakhan great in regard to homophobia? No. Is he great regarding patriarchy? No. Is he great regarding keeping track of the humanity of Jewish brothers and sisters? No. Is he great in terms of fighting white supremacy? Yes. He devoted his whole life to keeping track of white supremacy, and its effects and consequences as he understands them. He has been willing to live and die to uplift black people.

◆

American culture seems to lack two elements that are basic to racial justice: a deep sense of the tragic and a genuine grasp of the unadulterated rage directed at American society. The chronic refusal of most Americans to acknowledge the sheer absurdity that a person of African descent confronts in this country—the incessant assaults on black intelligence, beauty, character, and possibility—is not simply a matter of defending white-skin privilege. It also bespeaks a reluctance to look squarely at the brutality and tragedy of the American past and present.

Such a long and hard look would puncture the life-sustaining bubble of many Americans, namely that this nation of freedom-loving people and undeniable opportunity has committed unspeakable crimes against other human beings, especially black people.

◆

Reverend Jeremiah Wright is my dear brother. Recently he has been anointed as the media's latest incarnation of the "bad" Negro. Whether in slavery or in black communities under Jim Crow—bad Negroes are "out of control." Jeremiah Wright speaks his mind. Remember, all of us are cracked vessels. Jeremiah Wright deserves criticism, but it should be justifiable criticism. For example, Reverend Wright's claims about AIDS and HIV are wrong.

I've had the opportunity to speak in Reverend Wright's church on many occasions. I'm so glad whenever his full quote is played or published because any God worthy of worship condemns injustice. When he says, God damn America—killing innocent people. God damn America for treating her citizens as less than human. That is true for any nation. We must never put the cross under the flag.

Wright is a prophetic Christian preacher, therefore to him every flag is subordinate to the cross. If you believe that America has never killed innocent people, then God never damns America. We know God damns slavery, Jim and Jane Crow, the hatred of gays and lesbians, anti-Semitism, and anti-Arab "terror" bias in America. God is a God of justice and love.

What Wright was trying to address is the degree to which there is still injustice in America. *Never confuse this criticism with anti-Americanism.* Any resistance to injustice, be it in America, Egypt, Cuba, or Saudi Arabia, is a God-driven activity because righteous indignation against the cruel treatment of any group of people is an echo of the voice of God for those of us who take the cross seriously.

◆

Martin Luther King, Jr., made it quite clear when he said, *The criminal slaughter of the Vietnamese, especially the children, is a sign of American barbarity,* and that America was the greatest purveyor of violence in the 60s. Most importantly, on April 7, 1968, three days after his murder, King had planned to preach on "Why America May Go to Hell," but he would have said it with genuine agony and anguish.

The difference between Martin Luther King, Jr., and Jeremiah Wright is that Martin had a deep, unconditional love in him. He spoke in a style where you could almost see the tears flowing from his eyes. He empathized not just with those dealing with catastrophic circumstances but with the very folk who were ruling.

He knew that even rulers who are governed by greed and hatred must reap what they sow. In that sense, chickens do come home to roost. That's true for elites, be they in the Arab, European, Asian, African, or American world.

◆

During slavery, it was against the law for black people to learn how to read and write. Then came Jim Crow. Black people paid taxes for public institutions of higher learning but couldn't even think of sending their children to those institutions. Now, after finally getting a toehold during the civil rights era and gaining the right to attend previously segregated schools, we have an invisible tipping point. As soon as the black folk show up and begin to compete for previously uncontested resources, there's a national debate about black academic deficiencies and how rigorous standards must be enforced. That's a level of hypocrisy we ought to be honest about.

If students don't meet minimal qualifications, they don't belong. But let's understand how the white supremacist legacy influences the debate. How many students in any talent pool meet the shifting qualifications? My God, at Harvard 5,000 candidates do. Yet they only have 1,678 slots. So how do you work that out? Ted Kennedy barely met minimal qualifications. When he was granted admission to Harvard, he took some Irish working-class brother's slot who was brilliant and ended up at Boston College. I've said this to brother Kennedy—whose struggle for justice is legendary too— so I'm not speaking behind his back.

Kennedy knows his admission to Harvard was slam-dunked by legacy—son of, grandson of, brother of. When Ted showed up, was there a national debate broadcast around the world, in every corner of the globe, about the deficiency of rich Irish folk? No! When George Bush showed up at Yale, was there a debate about the qualifications of rich WASPS? No!

But let Jamal and Letitia show up, then the whole machinery of privilege kicks in, and suddenly everybody's deeply concerned about 780 college board scores or above. If you let Jamal and Letitia in—we're going to sue you! We should keep in mind that the white citizens who sued the University of Michigan in 2003 could have chosen white students who had much lower board scores too. They didn't. They chose to make their case against Negroes. What's really going on? Reverse racism? No. Plain old hypocrisy plus the legacy of white supremacy. Let's be honest about it.

◆

Historically, the progress of people of African descent in this country tends to go hand-in-hand with the unleashing of new opportunities for people far outside the black community, from women to people of color, to the handicapped, to the elderly, and so forth. Yet this does not occur easily. Somebody has to stand up and fight for it.

◆

Jefferson's notion of periodic revolution every generation or two, which one finds in the Declaration of Independence—may have unappreciated merit. I believe that people's accountability should be enforced by a radically changing and dynamic American democracy.

It is one of those moments in the Declaration of Independence that people aren't comfortable with.

They say, *Jefferson, you had your revolution, that's enough!*

Jefferson says: *No, we need to be renewed.*

In 1969, the Black Panthers used to sit in front of state capitals and read that portion of the Declaration of Independence—and it upset people. I heard Huey Newton read it when he was released from jail. People would say, *What revolutionary doctrine is he reading to us now?* It was Jefferson's Declaration of Independence.

◆

The culture of consumption has produced the highest level of self-destruction known in black history. We must pay close attention to these demons at work—the demons of futility, despair, and emptiness joined with the institutional and structural marginalization of working class black people. For the first time in black history, there are no viable institutions and structures in black American life that can effectively transmit values like hope, virtue, and sacrifice—institutions that put the needs of others higher than those of oneself.

In the past, every day, students in black colleges were forced to sit in pews and educators like Benjamin Mays would get up and say, *You must give service to the race and struggle for justice for all!* Mays reminded the black bourgeoisie that even as they went out into the world they had a cause, they had an obligation, they had a duty to contribute to something beyond their own self-interest. Even if we regard this practice as narrow-minded or short-sighted—these students had an institution that was transmitting an essential set of values to them.

And it wasn't just black schools doing the work. We can talk about the black church, fraternities, and sororities. We can talk about a whole host of other institutions in black civil society. **Today our institutions are being eroded slowly but surely.** This is what makes this era so terrifying.

This is why we have escalating black homicides that elevate the most cold-hearted, mean-spirited dispositions, and attitudes displayed by black people against other black people and non-blacks. This is why we have black suicides between ages 18 and 35 exponentially increasing—at unprecedented numbers in black history. Our moral fabric is being torn apart and shredded before our eyes.

◆

Some folk like Thomas Sowell and a host of others, such as Bill Cosby and Juan Williams, have said that there's something fundamentally different about black America now. They highlight the loss of values. Yet they somehow regard the loss of values as simple choices made by individuals, as though individuals are not shaped by the larger structural and institutional realities in our society.

These larger structures affect America as a whole, not just black America. But the negative consequences of structural breakdown tend to be concentrated among those who have less access to financial and psychological resources.

◆

If black people have learned anything, it is this: America is a profoundly conservative country, even with its commitment to experimentation and improvisation. By conservative, I mean its unwillingness to give up racism, sexism, and homophobia—and especially vast wealth inequality.

◆

Any time we talk about the black very poor, black poor and black working poor, we are describing the human beings who make up the so-called black underclass—outcasts in our society. These relatively invisible people live lives of economic and educational deprivation, and political marginalization in the richest nation in the history of the world.

The black underclass is a symbol for anarchy, social breakdown, social decay, the justification of law and order policies, and deep repressive tactics that go way beyond what is necessary for controlling crime or children.

There is an irony here. On one hand, the plight of the black underclass is invisible. On the other hand, its individual presence is highly visible on the six o'clock news in terms of violence. It is a way of instilling deep fear in the mainstream population, hence the incarceration of so many young people from the underclass. The issue is not just disgraceful schools, lack of healthcare or childcare, and no living wage jobs. There's also an unjust criminal justice system with differential treatment of majority versus minority drug habits—white middle-class cocaine versus ghetto crack.

◆

One-out-of-three black male babies today will grow up and spend time in jail or prison. That is a moral abomination! If there's not some serious focus on this reality as a *state of emergency*, as a matter of national security, then generations will be exiled to this new form of social death.

The prison-industrial complex, the major means by which the young black underclass is warehoused, has experienced exponential growth in prisoners—from less than a million 20-some years ago to 2.3 million prisoners today. We must do everything we can to guarantee that our criminal justice system is fair across the board. No matter who is on trial. The denial of the vote for ex-felons is a moral disgrace—a violation of democratic ideals.

There's a troubling paradox in terms of the invisibility and visibility of the underclass—our American outcasts. Unfortunately, we simply haven't had enough people to make their painful invisibility visible beyond the periodic incantations of crime and achievement-gap statistics.

The most demeaning images of the underclass are projected in the media 24/7. They are denied the right to be seen as human beings who are struggling in countless ways.

◆

Hip-hop, the most powerful cultural force on the globe right now, was one of the ways in which the black underclass responded to being forgotten and overlooked, with its pain downplayed and ignored.

The response to invisibility was to create a whole cultural genre that represented young, black, and underclass folk. The culture and entertainment industry had to take notice by 1985. Now hip-hop is the most lucrative cultural area of the entertainment industry. It's another tribute to the tremendous cultural imagination and genius of black folk.

Hip-hop was a particular response of a slice of the black underclass to (1) overcome their social misery, (2) sustain some sanity and dignity in their rituals with their Friday and Saturday night parties, and (3) try to keep alive a black musical tradition.

Louis Armstrong, who grew up in the red-light district of Storyville among the prostitutes and brothels, was able to escape the social misery and express his unbelievable genius and imagination to keep alive the greatest musical tradition of the modern world. The black musical tradition gave us blues and jazz idioms that the rest of the world now understands. Hip-hop, like the blues and jazz, came out of the black underclass. No other class in America can claim to have created the most important cultural force on the globe.

◆

America has intervened militarily in Latin America over 100 times in the last 162 years. It's going to be difficult for the government to somehow counter terrorism with democracy when it instituted militaristic policies that often reinforced antidemocratic regimes and sometimes overthrew democratic regimes.

National security has become more than an elastic term—it now justifies American imperial aggression and preemptive invasions and war in the name of democracy.

Tyranny can never be promoted as democracy.

◆

The American Empire is still governed by its desire to shape the world for American interests. It is still determined to have its way and do whatever it takes to preserve the resources necessary to sustain the "American way of life." Four dollar a gallon gasoline? Open the world's pipelines now—because it's all about us, all the time. America 2008 means obscene wealth and inequality, a political system characterized by legalized bribery and normalized corruption, a market-driven culture that tries to turn its citizens into sleepwalkers so they see themselves as consumers instead of citizens.

The new American Dream is to never run out of things to buy and sell, and people to buy and sell to. What must happen for us to stay awake permanently and commit to critically engaging the public interest or expanding the common good?

> To be human
> you must bear witness to justice.
> Justice is what love looks like in public—
> to be human is to love
> and be loved.

CHAPTER ELEVEN

FREEDOM

There is moral substance in the fact
that human will can make the future
different
and possibly better.

To deny death is to deny history, reality, and mortality. We're most human when we bury our dead, when we stand before the corpses of our loved ones, forced to bring together the three dimensions of time: past, present, and future.

In talking about cultural freedom we have to talk seriously about the various forms of death in our midst—past, present, and future. This allows us to do what? To become more alive, to think more critically, maybe be more compassionate, maybe even muster the courage to want to sacrifice for something bigger than us.

◆

I come from a particular tradition of struggle. My people have been on intimate terms with the constant threat of social death. No legal status, no social standing, no public value—you were only a commodity to be bought and sold. If you don't come to terms with death in that context, there's no way you can live psychically and culturally because the rights and privileges that your fellow human beings of European descent had access to were stripped from you.

◆

You remember Malcolm X's technical definition of a nigger. He said a nigger is a victim of American democracy. That was his formulation. It sounds oxymoronic. How can there be victims of American democracy? Well, there have been. Jeffersonian democracy pushed black folk further back and consolidated slavery. Poor whites in the South moved to the center. However, our American Indian brothers and sisters have been the ultimate victims of American democracy.

Even today, American democracy is expanding for certain folk and curtailed for others. Yet, the irony is that only more democracy can improve the plight of the victims of American democracy.

◆

Many people feel they no longer have to work or sacrifice. Why? Because the big money can be achieved right now.

◆

If you view yourself as part of a freedom-fighting tradition, part of those who live with their backs against the wall, you actually become willing to live and die for that struggle. This is why forms of intellectual weaponry become crucial, because you can begin to understand that what you're up against is easily a question of life and death.

The real danger is that traditions of freedom-fighting will slowly but surely disappear in our culture of consumption. The very possibility of a different future, the very possibility of a sense of hope for a society that's better than the present one will slowly but surely wane. In that kind of society, I'm not willing to live.

◆

I think highly of the pacifist tradition in Christendom. I do not agree with it. I am not persuaded by it. But I think respect is due. I do not think Christian pacifists will ever have the kind of impact on history that many of them profess to have. Yet I respect their views. So when I hear Archbishop Tutu and many others argue for nonviolence, I respect them.

One should, on principled ground, attempt to exercise and realize all forms of nonviolent resistance before one even remotely considers the discussion of violent resistance and armed struggle. One must examine the history of a country carefully and see what possibilities there have been for nonviolent resistance and what impact nonviolent resistance has had.

If we, in fact, discover that nonviolent resistance in its most noble form has been crushed mercilessly by the rulers, then it raises the possibility of forced engagement in armed struggle. Indeed, this is in no way alien to the Christian tradition. On the other hand, one should never view armed struggle as a plaything. One should not romanticize or idealize it at all. On the contrary, one should carefully and thoroughly think through whether it can have the impact and effectiveness that one desires.

As freedom fighters,
we've got to become much like
the jazz women and jazz men.
Fluid and flexible and protean——open to a variety
of different sources
and perspectives.

Black people's deep memory of history is a legacy of catastrophe. It's the slave ship and the body swinging from the tree. It's the disgraceful school systems and being taught to hate ourselves.

America's concept of history is that of a chosen people, a city on the hill where the sun is always shining. Therefore, black people's conception of memory is that of trauma, whereas the mainstream conception of memory is this progress of every generation toward a more perfect Union.

If your conception of history is one of catastrophe and your conception of memory is one of trauma, the only countermovement against catastrophe and trauma is *never forgetting* the catastrophic and yet still attempting to triumph.

You have to highlight what psychological, spiritual, cultural, political, and economic resources people had if you're going to deal with the catastrophic. You go to the spirituals, for example, during slavery. That's how, in part, black people were able to get over.

How did they love each other? By believing that God could love them—through song. Sometimes the people singing didn't even believe in God, but they knew it was empowering anyway. This is America. We crushed Jim Crow, Sr. and legalized segregation, American terrorism and lynching, but we know we still live with Jim Crow, Jr. today in terms of de facto segregation—where people live, who they associate with, who they socialize with, which press they read. There is still a sense that black people live in a very different world than the white mainstream, which is to say we live in both worlds. We read the *New York Times* and the *Washington Post.* Very few white brothers and sisters read the *Amsterdam News.* They don't read *Ebony.* They don't read *Jet.*

Look at the cover today of the *New York Times*, that beautiful picture of Frederick Douglass. What is America without Frederick Douglass? Not just because he's black, but because he's a democrat, small *d,* in a way in which the founding fathers were not. They were slaveholders, or "limited democrats." Theirs was a democracy for whites only.

Douglass says *No.* Martin says *No.* A. Philip Randolph says *No.* Ella Baker says *No.* This was key to American democracy: no habeas corpus, no due process or 14th Amendment without raising the question, What is the status of four million slaves?

When they finally raised the question, What is a citizen in America?, they had to answer that question in the 14th Amendment with another question: What is the status of our four million slaves? Black people's struggle for freedom is the key to the moral and political history of the democratic experiment called America.

This is the difference between our precious brown brothers and sisters, and our precious red and yellow brothers and sisters. Their presence and struggle for freedom does not have that particular weight and gravitas in the development of this precarious experiment called *democracy*.

◆

Oppressed people are preoccupied with survival rather than the struggle for freedom. They are thinking about the next day and the next week and the next month rather than some vision of emancipation. But when they decide to straighten their backs up, there is going to be a camp in every major American urban center. That camp meeting is going to signal the struggle for freedom with new energies, new possibilities unleashed, and the Lord's people better be ready to get on board. I am talking about getting ready, because it is coming. This is what the great Curtis Mayfield was talking about in his song "People Get Ready": The freedom train is coming!

◆

How do we radically reform a system while working within it? Given the fragmentation of the labor force, the de-skilling and re-skilling of workers due to the automation, computerization, robotization, and globalization in the workplace—who will become the major agents of social change? Who will set us free?

◆

Young people want total freedom and to make the easy buck now. In many ways they're mirroring what they see in society at large, what they see on Wall Street. It makes it very difficult for them to take seriously not only commitment and caring and sacrificing, but ultimately to take human life itself seriously. Profits become much more important than human life. What we see is a very cold-hearted mean-spiritedness throughout these communities. It reflects so much of our own culture and civilization. It's quite frightening.

> Subversive joy is the ability to transform tears into laughter,
> a laughter that allows one to acknowledge
> just how difficult the journey is,
> and to delight in one's own sense of
> humanity and folly and humor
> in the midst of this very serious struggle.
> This is true freedom of spirit.

We can think and feel, laugh and weep, and with the belief and capacity of everyday people, we can fight. Fight with a smile on our faces and tears in our eyes. We can see the deprivation, yet hold up a bloodstained banner with a sense of hope based on genuine discernment and connection. We can point out hypocrisy and keep alive some sense of possibility for both ourselves and our children, thus fulfilling our sacred duty.

The Adventures of Huck Finn, Chapter 31—it's one of the great sublime moments in American literature. Huck has to make the decision, when he takes the letter and rips it up and says, "Alright, then, I'll go to hell." He knows his soul is going to hell and he's going to resist civilization. He's going to resist the various kinds of sanctions that his aunt put on him. He takes a stand for integrity and conscience. It's not even a political act. It's just a moral shaping of his soul. It's an attempt to become more mature.

He'd rather go to hell than deny the humanity of Nigger Jim and he recognizes that niggerization is a lie.

It's an unbelievable discovery for a white person. It's a breakhrough. *This Jim, who's been niggerized, is a human being and I can revel in his humanity. I need him and he needs me as a co-participant in the shaping of what is to be America and democratic.*

That's a great moment. That's Samuel Clemens.

◆

I'm sometimes accused of being anti-American, and I just say that as Plato attempted to make the world safe for Socrates,

I'm attempting to make the world safe for the legacy of Martin Luther King, Jr.—and King was the best of America!

It's fascinating
the degree to which
black people in America
provide one of the fundamental keys to the future,
if the future is going to be about
freedom and equality.

Freedom is an awakening from sleepwalking. Any such awakening is like falling in love—you begin to care so much that you can't help yourself. That is why the most desirable and wise way of living—*a life of radical love in freedom and radical freedom in love*—lures us to fall awake in order to stand for something bigger and grander than ourselves. Did not Rosa Parks fall awake on that bus in Montgomery to take a stand for truth and justice?

© Jeffry Andres Wright

CHAPTER TWELVE

WISDOM

The battle is perennial; yet each of us in our time must fight.

◆

If you live long enough, a moment of spiritual death is inevitable. The question is: How will you wrestle with it?

Jesus experienced spiritual death on the cross. Abandoned by the most powerful force in the universe, he cried out,

"My God, my God, why hast thou forsaken me?"

You can't talk about the crucifixion without talking about nihilism and spiritual abandonment. The feeling that you have no connection whatsoever to any of the forces for good in the universe underscores your relatively helpless situation.

If Jesus had American advisors, they would have said, *Negotiate with Pontius Pilate, sacrifice your sense of who you are, call your mission into question, and sneak away at night under the protective cover of the Roman Empire to live free.*

Jesus would have responded, *No, there's a cross for me. In fact, if you look closely enough in your life, there's a cross for you, too.*

◆

Martin Luther King, Jr., following the great Benjamin E. Mays, used to say we are all part of one garment of destiny, one inextricable network of mutuality. We have to acknowledge that, whether we like each other or not.

◆

Traditionally, black people have labored under the false notion that we must be homogeneous to be strong. They confused homogeneity with unity. Strong unity actually comes from affirming our diversity.

> Democracy does not romanticize or idealize everyday people.
> Instead, it recognizes each person's potential and possibility,
> as well as his or her limitations.

We should never be arrogant enough to think that we can create some kind of critique-free situation. Neither should we despair because we are human and therefore inadequate, thinking that we don't have the capacity to be better.

◆

Eugene O'Neill said it so well in an interview prior to the first production of the great American play *The Iceman Cometh* in 1946. He acknowledges that Americans suffer from this notion that somehow they can possess their souls by means of possessing commodities.

Oh, Eugene, we need you, we need you, brother! Your insight still ripples down through these 62 years, revealing an empire that has the capacity to conquer the world but has completely lost its soul.

It's no accident that Martin Luther King, Jr. and the Southern Leadership Christian Conference chose the motto *"To save the soul of America,"* which became the theme of the freedom movement. He didn't have to read *The Iceman Cometh* to know what Eugene O' Neill was talking about.

Is everything here
up for sale?
No democracy can survive
in that context.

No empire lasts forever. All empires come and go. They ebb and flow. Chickens do come home to roost. Sooner or later reality is going to help you reap what you sow.

◆

There will be no significant change in the situation of poor people—especially poor people of color—without transracial and interracial coalition and alliance. Black folk cannot do it alone.

◆

The attempt to make the government responsible to disadvantaged citizens is an idea that will never go away in the modern world. Over the last twenty years, in part because of corporate domination of the economy and government, the programs we have designed have provided very limited benefits for the poor.

◆

America is an immature culture. Its obsession with innocence, refusal to look at darkness, and sentimental disposition toward itself and the world has made it impossible to come to terms with catastrophic circumstances. All of our talk about the suffering of red, black, or working peoples, or women, gays, and lesbians, still too often leaves us incapable of telling the truth.

If it is true that black people are becoming increasingly well adjusted to the American way of life, then we may lose our capacity to tell the truth about our black life in America.

There's a political front and a cultural front. Think about when Martin Luther King began to critique American imperialism in his speeches against the Vietnam War. The vast majority of black people and leaders rejected what he had to say and trashed his formulations.

Even though he was still loved as a leader in the face of white supremacy, once he connected white supremacy at home to American imperialism abroad, black folk couldn't take it.

Their patriotism would not allow it. Their fear of being branded as traitors to America was too overwhelming, so they began to distance themselves from him.

That was true for moderate black leaders like Whitney Young and Roy Wilkins as well as for millions of everyday black folk on the ground. When Martin was murdered the black masses were still ignorant of the depth of his critique of Vietnam, but he inhabited the heart and soul of black America. They loved him so deeply that their rage and anguish spilled over, 125 rebellions in 29 states were unleashed and over 100,000 federal troops were deployed all around the country.

◆

In his autobiography, James Brown says "Martin was America's best friend." America would never have made it into a post-apartheid state in the South without Martin's gentle spirit, loving orientation, and his willingness to embrace even those who were engineering his death. How many of us could carry that cross?

◆

In the end, what if all Americans really want is material prosperity and personal security?

What if we have been so thoroughly misshaped by the new American dream—our disposable, buy-and-sell celebrity culture that, like Gatsby, if we can't have it, we'd rather change our identity or die. Maybe America no longer wants moral magnanimity and personal integrity. That is mighty deep, but if it's true—who's going to pay the bill?

◆

In the light of the present, what do we see? One of the bleakest moments in the history of world civilization. America is the last and only grand Empire. In scope, in depth, in power it exceeds the British *and* the Roman Empires. There has never been anything like it in the history of humankind.

There are no countervailing forces opposing the American Empire. The oppressive Soviet Empire went under seventeen years ago. It was the only countervailing force.

Like all Empires, the American Empire is arrogant. It's blind and believes it can shape the world in its own image, dictating its terms according to its unbridled desires. My dear brother, Noam Chomsky, reminds us that our empire has advanced a new doctrine of preemptive strike. Do unto your enemies before they do unto you—i.e., if you claim that someone's about to attack you then you attack them first.

Unfortunately, that cowboy posturing obscures the real doctrine, which says that if some nation has a group of elites that are contemplating a challenge to U.S. power, it's subject to attack.

That's "preventive" war—the new precedent in international relations. It's the law of the jungle. It sends ill-advised signals, like troops in a hundred nations, bases in seventy nations, a major carrier in every ocean. Domestically, two percent of the population owns 51 percent of the wealth. Five percent owns 70 percent of the wealth, and that's before Bush's tax cuts.

◆

In the face of the Patriot Act I, the Patriot Act II, escalating authoritarianism, the violation of rights and liberties, we must keep smiling, keep fighting, keep thinking, keep loving, keep serving, and keep sacrificing. It's not about the overnight win, it's not about the quick fix, it's not about the pushbutton solution. It's about what kind of human being you choose to be and what kind of legacy you want to live.

◆

In the darkness, you begin to see more clearly those who have been telling the truth, exposing lies, and bearing witness. People who you thought were telling the truth get exposed. People who you thought were lying get exposed. People you thought were really bearing witness get exposed as folk just keeping a job and making money.

◆

Freedom fighters struggle for justice, not revenge. We love in the face of bigotry. We keep track of the indescribable scars and bruises. Yet we refuse to be victims! We instead mount constant heroic resistance against injustice.

◆

We can learn white supremacy, male supremacy, homophobia, imperial arrogance. We can learn that the world is or isn't flat.

However, to overcome that kind of ignorance, we must be open to the force of criticism.

◆

None of us is in any way free of spot or wrinkle as earthly vessels while we struggle in this battle against racism. This is one of the most critical issues that needs to be discussed in America, so we can create bonds of trust and understanding.

We can't go into these dialogues finger-pointing. People have to be true to themselves while simultaneously holding one unshakable conviction—*I am willing to struggle against all forms of racism until the day I die.*

An opinion
is a deed.

During the Bush administration, those in high places have been fiddling while the empire burns. Those who dared to speak the truth loudly, clearly, and lucidly began to energize and galvanize folk who would not ordinarily believe themselves capable of turning the tide. Because that is what it's going to take.

◆

There is always a fundamental tension between a commitment to truth and a quest for power. The two are never compatible. It could be Socrates, Jesus, Martin Luther King, Jr., or Fannie Lou Hamer. You always need a prophetic critique of those in power. Power intoxicates. Power seduces. Power corrupts. Absolute power corrupts absolutely. There is always a need for somebody to tell the truth to the powerful.

Half-truths are dangerous—
they mystify, they conceal,
but do they say enough about
the "real" to seduce us?

I tell Brother Obama, "Brother, do not confuse mature courage and blues hope with adolescent bravery and naïve audacity." They are not the same.

Look at the hope in blues people. Look at the Irish with the British. Look at Jewish folk in Jew-hating Europe. They were never optimistic. They were hopeful that their children would go against the grain and muster the love and will to resist.

◆

When you talk about hope, you have to be a long distance runner. This is again so very difficult in our culture, because the quick fix, the overnight solution militate against being a long distance runner in the moral sense—the sense of fighting because it is right, because it is moral, because it is just. Hope linked to combative spirituality is what I have in mind.

◆

Remember what the great Rabbi Abraham Joshua Heschel said about indifference? The indifference to evil is more insidious than the evil itself. That's very strong language, but it's a true possibility. America cannot stand another 10 to 15 years of an Ice Age. It cannot stand it. If justice is what love looks like in public, then deep democracy is what justice looks like in practice.

◆

To be modern is to be suspicious of authority telling you how to choose. The church isn't going to tell me how to choose, momma isn't going to tell me, daddy isn't going to tell me—because a lot of these authorities have really made a wreck of the world.

I must ask myself how I will choose. It requires self-trust and self-reliance. No authority, no tradition, nothing external to me is going to tell me how to choose. It's just me, myself, and I. The irony is, if the only authority is the self, then will that also make a wreck of the world?

◆

The fundamental irony of American history is that we follow the better angels of our nature when we honestly and compassionately confront the devilish realities we would like to ignore or deny.

◆

Most new people come to the U.S. and overlook America's dark side. They move into immigrant status and then work very hard at gaining access to these unbelievable opportunities. As far as it goes, that's beautiful. I celebrate that. But what about the dreams of hardworking, undocumented immigrants?

◆

The U.S. Constitution was, in practice, a pro-slavery document for nearly a century. To put it crudely, the deep democratization of America was pitted against the ugly niggerization in America.

◆

Niggerization is neither simply the dishonoring and devaluing of black people, nor solely the economic exploitation and political disenfranchisement of them. It is also the wholesale attempt to impede democratization.

◆

Since the ugly events of 9/11 and Katrina, we have witnessed the attempt of the Bush administration—with elites in support and populists complacent—to promote the niggerization of the American people.

◆

The future of the American idea—both then and now, here and abroad—depends on the vision, courage, and determination of decent and compassionate people to engage in Socratic questioning of the powers that be, to take the risk of prophetic witness and to preserve a hope for democratization.

> The American practice
> of niggerization
> must die
> for the American idea
> of democratization
> to live——yet again.

People cannot live on arguments. They might be influenced by arguments, but they don't live on arguments. They live on love, care, respect, touch, and so forth.

◆

We have to keep track of every social movement by calculating who is bearing most of the social cost. This is what it means to look at the world from the vantage point of those below.

Democratization is the best
of all American ideals—
in principle and practice.

Whether or not my brother Barack Obama wins the presidential election, he has won the historical moment. His undeniable victory is to shatter the racist glass ceiling that enshrined America's most sacred office and to inspire millions here and abroad that a new day in America is possible. Yet it remains unclear whether America has the capacity to treat the masses of everyday black people equally or decently.

Obama's brilliance, charisma and organizational genius have been a grand catalyst for hope. The verdict is not yet in whether he can maintain his hope on a tightrope.

◆

When we look at our past, we do not fantasize, we do not idealize, but we also do not succumb to the narrow view that we have done nothing. Somewhere amidst our struggle, we've won, we've lost, we've cried, we've laughed, we've had love and joy, we've had sorrow and peace. Although great damage has been done, ours is not a history solely of oppression. Ours is not a history solely of futile resistance. Indeed some great world-changing victories have been won.

Those who have never despaired have neither lived nor loved. Hope is inseparable from despair. Those of us who truly hope make despair a constant companion whom we outwrestle every day owing to our commitment to justice, love, and hope. It is impossible to look honestly at our catastrophic conditions and not have some despair—it is a healthy sign of how deeply we care. It is also a mark of maturity—a rejection of cheap American optimism.

To be wise is to opt for a costly hope, an earned hope, a blues-inflected hope that grapples with despair. Yet like Jacob wrestling with the angel of darkness in the midnight hour in Genesis 32:34, we emerge with new energy from our wounds, new wisdom from our scars, and a new name from our bruises, equipped with a new armor of truth and justice.

Wisdom comes from wrestling with despair and not allowing despair to have the last word. That's why hope is always blood-stained and tear-soaked.

The fundamental question for the wise person is: How do we wounded and scarred creatures choose to be wounded-healers, not wounded-hurters, or scarred-helpers, not scarred-playahaters? And hope gives us strength to try to have it so—to try to keep struggling for more love, more justice, more freedom, and more democracy.

For me—as a Christian—since Jesus dropped the charges at the cross—I choose to be a free black man who is willing to live and die for truth and justice, love and democracy, regardless of what the world gives or takes away!

WESTIAN CORE CONCEPTS

Blues—The elegant coping with catastrophe that yields a grace and dignity so that the spirit of resistance is never completely snuffed out.

Constantinian Christianity—Christian faith and practice well-adjusted to greed, hatred, and fear.

Deep democracy—The courage to lift our voices and have them heard in order to shape our destiny.

Small *d* democrats—Those who focus on the most vulnerable among us when we talk about public interest and common good.

Freedom fighters—Fanatics for fairness and extremists of love.

Gangsterization of America—The unaccountable overflow of greed, hatred, and fear in every sphere of the country.

Market culture, marketplace culture, market-driven culture—Ways of living and being obsessed with immediate pleasure, immense property, and impressive power for personal gain.

Niggerization—A uniquely American process that tries to keep Black people so scared, intimidated, helpless, and hopeless that they give up, cave in, or sell out in the fight for justice, love, and hope.

Paideia—Deep education that informs and transforms us so we shift from bling bling to a quest for wisdom.

Post-modern—The age of the American Empire alongside corporate globalization.

Prophetic Christianity—Christian faith and practice maladjusted to greed, hatred, and fear that bears the fruits of justice, love, and hope.

Prophetic thinkers—Intellectuals willing to live and die for justice, love, and hope.

White supremacist slavery—244 years of dehumanizing black people based on white greed, hatred, and fear. Only the fight for justice, love, and hope rescued America from chaos.

THE **BOOKS** AND **MUSIC** THAT **MADE ME**

I am often asked which books I love and which music I listen to. Those books that most influence me are food to my soul. I read and reread them—as they read and reread me. But I cannot mention the influence of books without acknowledging the impact of music. In fact, I believe that music is deeper than philosophy, Beethoven deeper than Goethe or Hegel, Coltrane deeper than Du Bois or Ellison. So I provide a brief selection of my favorite books and music—the intellectual and visceral stuff that helps me sustain my hope on a tightrope.

BOOKS

Anton Chekhov, *Collected Short Stories* and *Collected Plays*

William Shakespeare, *Hamlet, King Lear, The Tempest, King John*

Thomas Hardy, *Collected Poems*

Toni Morrison, *Beloved* and *Playing in the Dark*

Ivan Turgenev, *Fathers and Sons*

Leo Tolstoy, *War and Peace* and *How Much Land Does a Man Need?*

Plato, *The Republic, The Symposium, Apology, Phaedo, Timaeus*

Sophocles, *Antigone* and *Oedipus at Colonus*

Dante, *Inferno*

Lucian, "Philosophers for Sale" in *The Selected Satires of Lucian*

Richard Wright, *Native Son* and *12 Million Black Voices*

Muriel Rukeyser, *The Life of Poetry*

Sappho, *Poems*

Miguel de Cervantes, *Don Quixote*

Erasmus, *In Praise of Folly*

Ralph Ellison, *Invisible Man* and *Shadow and Act*

Fyodor Dostoevsky, *The Brothers Karamazov*

Guy de Maupassant, *Collected Stories*

W.E.B. Du Bois, *The Souls of Black Folk*

Friedrich Nietzsche, *Twilight of the Idols*

Arthur Schopenhauer, *Essays and Aphorisms*

Ralph Waldo Emerson, *Collected Essays*

Voltaire, *Candide*

Immanuel Kant, *What is Enlightenment?* and *Kant on History and Religion,* "On the Failure of All Attempted Philosophical Theodicies"

Virginia Woolf, *A Room of One's Own*

Georg Christoph Lichtenberg, *Aphorisms*

Jonathan Swift, *A Tale of a Tub*

Herman Melville, *The Confidence Man* and *Moby Dick*

Georg Hegel, *Lectures on the History of Philosophy*

David Hume, *Dialogues Concerning Natural Religion*

Thomas Mann, *Doctor Faustus*

James Baldwin, *The Price of the Ticket (Collected Prose)*

Henrik Ibsen, *A Doll's House, The Wild Duck, John Gabriel Borkman*

Erich Auerbach, *Mimesis*

George Steiner, *Antigones*

M.H. Abrams, *Natural Supernaturalism*

T.S. Eliot, *The Wasteland* and *Four Quartets*

Blaise Pascal, *Pensées*

Leroi Jones (Amiri Baraka), *Blues People: Negro Music in White America*

Tennessee Williams, *A Streetcar Named Desire* and *Cat on a Hot Tin Roof*

Thomas Pynchon, *Gravity's Rainbow*

Samuel Beckett, *Waiting for Godot* and *Worstward Ho!*

Federico García Lorca, *Collected Poems* and *Plays*

Nikos Kazantzakis, *Christ Recrucified*

Frantz Kafka, *The Metamorphosis, The Penal Colony, A Hunger Artist*

Nathanael West, *Miss Lonelyhearts*

Pablo Neruda, *Collected Poems*

Eugene O'Neill, *The Iceman Cometh* and *Long Day's Journey into Night*

Edward Said, *The World, the Text and the Critic*

C. Wright Mills, *The Sociological Imagination*

Derek Walcott, *Collected Poems*

Wole Soyinka, *Myth, Literature and the African World* and *Death and the King's Horseman*

Martin Luther King, Jr., *Strength to Love*

Frantz Fanon, *The Wretched of the Earth*

George Santayana, Collected philosophy and poetry

MUSIC

John Coltrane—whole corpus, especially *Giant Steps* (Atlantic 1960), *My Favorite Things* (Atlantic 1961), *A Love Supreme* (Impulse 1965)

Sarah Vaughan—whole corpus, especially "Send in the Clowns," "Body and Soul"

Marvin Gaye—whole corpus, especially *What's Going On* (Motown 1971), *Lets Get It On* (Motown 1973), *Live! At the London Palladium* (Tamla 1977)

Stevie Wonder—whole corpus, especially *Talking Book* (Motown 1972), *Songs in the Key of Life* (Motown 1976), "Superstition"

Curtis Mayfield—whole corpus, especially *Greatest Hits:* "I Love and I Lost," We're a Winner," "I'm So Proud," "The Makings of You"

James Brown—whole corpus, especially *Live at the Apollo* (6/25/67); *Greatest Hits:* "Soul Power," "Make It Funky," "There It Is," "Papa Don't Take No Mess," "Superbad," "Funk On a Roll"

Aretha Franklin—whole corpus, especially *Amazing Grace* (Atlantic 1972); *Greatest Hits,* especially "Daydreaming," "Say a Little Prayer," "Respect," "Rock Steady," "I Never Loved a Man"

The Dramatics—*Greatest Hits,* especially "Fall in Love, Lady Love," "Thank You For Your Love," "In the Rain," "Fell for You," "Welcome Back Home," "You're the Best Thing in My Life"

The Whispers—*Greatest Hits,* especially "Chocolate Girl," "Lady," "You Are Number One"

LeVert—*Greatest Hits,* especially "All Seasons," "Smile," "Casanova," "Good Stuff"

Al Green—*Greatest Hits,* especially "Let's Stay Together," "Everything Gonna Be Alright," "I'm So Tired of Being Alone"

The Stylistics—*Greatest Hits,* especially "Payback is a Dog," "Peek A Boo," "Betcha By Golly, Wow," "Hurry Up This Way Again"

Blue Magic—*The Best of Blue Magic,* especially "Chasing Rainbows," "The Loneliest House on the Block," "Three Ring Circus," "What's Come Over Me?"

The Main Ingredient—*A Quiet Storm* (RCA 1996), especially "You've Been My Inspiration," "It's So Sweet (Loving You)," "You've Got to Take It (If You Want It)," "I'm Leaving This Time"

The Chi-Lites—*Greatest Hits* (Brunswick 1998), especially "The Coldest Days of My Life," "A Letter to Myself," "Toby," "Have You Seen Her?"

Enchantment—*The Best of Enchantment* (EMI Latin 1996), especially "It's You That I Need," "Gloria," "Sunshine," "Silly Love Song"

Ashford and Simpson—*The Very Best of Ashford and Simpson* (Rhino 2002), especially "(I'd Know You) Anywhere," "It Seems to Hang On," "Is it Still Good to Ya?" "Solid"

Ella Fitzgerald—whole corpus, especially *Ella Sings Gershwin* (Decca 1946), *Ella Fitzgerald Sings the Cole Porter Songbook* (Polygram 1956)

Carmen McRae—whole corpus, especially "What Are You Doing the Rest of Your Life?" "There's No Such Thing as Love"

Teddy Pendergrass—*Greatest Hits* (The Right Stuff 1998), especially "Come Go With Me," "Love TKO," "When Somebody Loves You Back," "You're My Latest, Greatest Inspiration"

Donny Hathaway—*A Donny Hathaway Collection* (Atlantic/WEA 1990), especially "Someday We'll All Be Free," "The Ghetto," "To Be Young, Gifted and Black," "A Song for You"

Maze, featuring Frankie Beverly—*Greatest Hits,* especially "Joy and Pain," "Before I Let Go," "We Are One"

Luther Vandross—*Hits,* especially "Any Love," "So Amazing," "Don't Want to Be a Fool," "A House Is Not a Home"

Gladys Knight and The Pips—*The Best of Gladys Knight and the Pips* (Sony 2001), especially "Neither One of Us," "You're the Best Thing that Ever Happened to Me," "Still Such a Thing"

The Temptations—whole corpus, especially *Love Songs* (Motown 2004; recorded 1965–1975), especially "You're My Everything," "Heavenly," "Just My Imagination," "My Girl"

Lou Rawls—*Greatest Hits* (Curb 1990), especially "Lady Love," "Love Is a Hurtin' Thing"

LTD—*The Best of LTD,* especially "Love Ballad," "We Both Deserve Each Other's Love," "You'll Never Find a Love Like Mine"

Smokey Robinson and the Miracles—whole corpus, especially *Greatest Hits* (1996; Polygram UK 2005): "Choosey Beggar," "You Must Be Love," "What Love Has Joined Together," "More Love," "Ooo Baby Baby"

The Isley Brothers—whole corpus, especially *Greatest Hits* (Motown 1991): "For the Love of You," "Harvest for the World," "Caravan of Love," "(At Your Best) You Are Love," "Groove With You"

Earth, Wind and Fire—*Greatest Hits* (Sony 1998), especially "Devotion," "Reasons," "That's the Way of the World," "On Your Face"

The Spinners—*The Very Best of the Spinners* (Atlantic/WEA 1993), especially "How Could I Let You Get Away?" "Ghetto Child," "Could It Be I'm Falling in Love"

Sam Cooke—*Greatest Hits* (RCA 1998), especially "You Send Me," "A Change Is Gonna Come," "Cupid"

Glenn Jones—*Greatest Hits* (Razor & Tie 1998), especially "We've Only Just Begun," "Show Me," "Here I Go Again"

SOS Band—*The Best of SOS Band* (Tabour 1 France 1995), especially "Tell Me if You Still Care," "Weekend Girl," "The Finest"

Phillis Hyman—*Greatest Hits* (Arista 1989), especially "It's You," "Living Alone"

Jill Scott—*Greatest Hits,* especially "Family Reunion"

The Emotions—*Chronicle Greatest Hits* (Stax 1979), especially "Walking the Line," "So I Can Love You"

The Manhattans—*Love Songs* (Sony 2000), especially "Am I Losing You?" "Girl of My Dream," "It Feels So Good to Be Loved So Bad"

Stephanie Mills—*Greatest Hits: 1985–1993* (MCA 1996), especially "Something in the Way (You Make Me Feel)," "Secret Lady," "I Feel Good All Over"

El DeBarge—*Ultimate Collection* (Hip-O Records 2003), especially "Love Always," "Heart, Mind and Soul," "Broken Dreams"

Billy Stewart—*The Best of Billy Stewart* (MCA 2000), especially "I Do Love You," "Sitting in the Park"

Gene Chandler—*20 Greatest Hits* (Collectables 1994), especially "Just Be True," "Rainbow" (parts 1 & 2), "What Now?"

George Clinton—*500,000 Kilowatts of P-Funk Power* (Fruit Tree Italy 2004), especially "Standing on the Verge," "Make My Funk the P-Funk," "Flashlight"

Parliament Funkadelic—*Chocolate City* (Polygram 1975),
One Nation Under a Groove (1978; Priority Records 2002)

Otis Redding—*The Very Best of Otis Redding* (Elektra/WEA 1992),
especially "Try a Little Tenderness," "(Sittin' On) The Dock
of the Bay"

Freddie Jackson—*The Greatest Hits of Freddie Jackson* (Capitol 1994),
especially "Have You Ever Loved Somebody?" "Love is Just a
Touch Away," "I Don't Want To Lose Your Love"

Duke Ellington—his *entire* corpus, especially "Mood Indigo," "Take the
A Train," "Sophisticated Lady"

Louie Armstrong—his *entire* corpus, especially "West End Blues"

Sly and the Family Stone—*Greatest Hits* (1970; Sony 1990), especially
"Thank You (Falettinme Be Mice Elf Agin)," "Stand," "Everyday
People," "You Can Make It If You Try," "Everybody Is a Star"

Billie Holiday—*Greatest Hits* (Decca; Sony 1998), especially "God Bless
the Child," "Strange Fruit," "Body and Soul"

Ludwig van Beethoven—whole corpus, especially *Symphonies 3, 5, 6, 8
& 9*; *String Quartet*, op.131; *Piano Sonata No. 18*, op. 123; *Concerto in
D Major*, op. 61; *Missa Solemnis*, op. 13

James Cleveland—*Greatest Hits,* especially "This Too Will Pass,"
"Jesus Is the Best Thing That Happened to Me," "A Good Day"

Maxwell—*Maxwell's Urban Hang Suite* (Sony 1996)

Cameo—*Greatest Hits* (Polygram 1998), especially "Word Up," "She's
Strange," "Don't Be Lonely"

Barry White—*The Ultimate Collection* (Mercury 2000), especially
"Never, Never Gonna Give Ya Up," "Can't Get Enough of Your
Love, Babe"

Nat King Cole—*The Greatest Hits* (Capitol 1994), especially "The Very Thought of You," "My Love Is Here to Stay," "Unforgettable"

Wolfgang Amadeus Mozart—whole corpus, especially operas: *Don Giovanni*, K. 527, *The Marriage of Figaro*, K. 492, *The Magic Flute*, K. 620; symphonies: *No. 40 in G Minor*, K. 550, *No. 41 in C Minor*, K. 551

Stephen Sondheim—*Our Greatest Playwright in Song*, especially *A Little Night Music, Company, Follies, Sunday in the Park with George, Sweeney Todd, Passion*

Frank Sinatra—*Greatest Hits*, especially "Young at Heart," "In the Wee Wee Hours of the Night," "Send in the Clowns"

Sergei Rachmaninoff—*Concerto No. 2 in C Minor*, op. 18; *Rhapsody on a Theme of Paganini*, op. 43

Frederic Chopin—whole corpus, especially *Twenty-Four Preludes*, op. 28; *Polonaise-Fantaisie in A-flat Major*, op. 61

Con Funk Shun—*The Best of Con Funk Shun* (Island/Mercury 1993), especially "Love's Train"

Mary J. Blige—*Reflections: A Retrospective* (Geffen 2006), especially "Real Love"

Michael Jackson—whole corpus, especially *Off the Wall* (Epic 1979; Sony 2001), "Whose Loving You?" "Never Can Say Goodbye"

Prince—whole corpus, especially "Kiss," "Adore," "Sign 'O' The Times"

Oscar Peterson—whole corpus, especially *Oscar Peterson Plays the George Gershwin Songbook* (Polygram 1996)

Grandmaster Flash and the Furious Five—*Grandmaster Flash and the Furious Five* (Sequel Records UK 1994), especially "The Message"

Eric B. and Rakim—*Paid in Full* (1987; Fourth & Bway/PGD 1996)

Bob Marley—whole corpus, especially "Redemption Song," "No Woman No Cry"

Atlantic Starr—*Greatest Hits* (K-Tel 1997), especially "Secret Lovers," "Silver Shadow," "If Your Heart Isn't In It"

Mahalia Jackson—whole corpus, especially "Move on Up a Little Higher," "How I Got Over"

B.B. King—whole corpus, especially "I Got a Bad Case of Love," "The Thrill Is Gone"

Wynton Marsalis—whole corpus

Miles Davis—whole corpus, especially "Sketches of Spain," "A Kind of Blue"

Thelonious Monk—whole corpus, especially "Round Midnight," "Epistrophy"

Johannes Brahms—*Piano Concerto No. 2 in B-flat Minor*, op. 83; *A German Requiem*, op. 45

ACKNOWLEDGMENTS

This book is an expression of my vision and viewpoint fundamentally shaped by my precious family—the late Clifton L. West Jr. and Irene B. West, Clifton L. West III, Cheryl West, Cynthia McDaniel, Clifton L. West and Dilan Zeytun West.

This book is the brainchild of my adopted brother, Tavis Smiley, who came up with the idea and created the road of its journey. The editorial genius and spiritual depth of Cheryl Woodruff literally helped me put this book together—alongside her marvelous staff, especially the brilliant and dedicated B. Colby Hamilton and Diana Marie Delgado. A special thanks to Charles McStravick for his outstanding design. Needless to say, without the vision and support of my magnificent assistant, Mary Ann Rodriguez, this work would not exist.

My thanks also to my incomparable literary agent, Gloria Loomis, who has for nearly fifteen years exemplified the highest excellence. I am blessed to publish with SmileyBooks—a part of the grand project of love and service to everyday people—founded by the inimitable and incredible Tavis Smiley in cooperation with Hay House Publishers. We all have pledged our time and energy to sustain *Hope on a Tightrope*. And we intend to be faithful unto death!

Educator and philosopher Cornel West is the Class of 1943 University Professor at Princeton University. Known as one of America's most gifted, provocative, and important public intellectuals, he is the author of the contemporary classic *Race Matters,* which changed the course of America's dialogue on race and justice, and the *New York Times* bestseller *Democracy Matters.* He is the recipient of the American Book Award and holds more than 20 honorary degrees.